BEST
EDITORIAL
CARTOONS
OF THE YEAR

CHANGE

ANGELO
LOPEZ 2012

ANGELO LOPEZ
Courtesy Philippines Today

BEST EDITORIAL CARTOONS OF THE YEAR

2013 EDITION

Edited by
STEVE KELLEY

Text by
CHARLES G. BROOKS, JR.

PELICAN PUBLISHING COMPANY
Gretna 2013

Dedicated to the memory of Charles Brooks, Sr.,
who edited this series for forty years

Library of Congress Serial Catalog Data

Best Editorial Cartoons, 1972-
Gretna [La.] Pelican Pub. Co.
v. 41 cm annual—
"A pictorial history of the year."

United States—Politics and Government—
1969—Caricatures and Cartoons—Periodicals.
E839.5.B45 320.9'7309240207 73-643645
ISSN 0091-2220   MARC-S

Printed in the United States of America
Published by Pelican Publishing Company, Inc.
1000 Burmaster Street, Gretna, Louisiana 70053

Contents

Award-Winning Cartoons

2012 PULITZER PRIZE

MATT WUERKER

Editorial Cartoonist
Politico

Staff cartoonist for Politico since its founding in 2006; provides editorial cartoons, caricatures, illustrations, and web animations for print and web; twice a finalist for the Pulitzer Prize; winner of the Herblock Award for Cartooning and the National Press Foundation's Berryman Award, 2010.

2011 SIGMA DELTA CHI AWARD
(Selected in 2012)

MATT BORS

Editorial Cartoonist
Universal Uclick

Graduate of the Art Institute of Pittsburgh, 2003; cartoonist, journalist, and editor in Portland, Oregon; draws the weekly comic strip "Idiot Box"; his work appears in the anthology *Attitude 3: The New Subversive Online Cartoonist;* comics journalism editor for Cartoon Movement, which is devoted to international political cartooning; also winner of 2012 Herblock Award for Cartooning; work distributed by Universal Uclick.

2012 HERBLOCK AWARD

MATT BORS

Editorial Cartoonist
Universal Uclick

NICK ANDERSON

Editorial Cartoonist
Houston Chronicle

Native of Toledo, Ohio; graduate of The Ohio State University; editorial cartoonist for the *Louisville Courier-Journal,* 1991-2006, and the *Houston Chronicle,* 2006 to the present; previous winner of the John Fischetti Competition, 1999; also winner of the Sigma Delta Chi Award, 2000, and the Pulitzer Prize, 2005; syndicated by the Washington Post Writers Group.

2012 NATIONAL HEADLINER AWARD

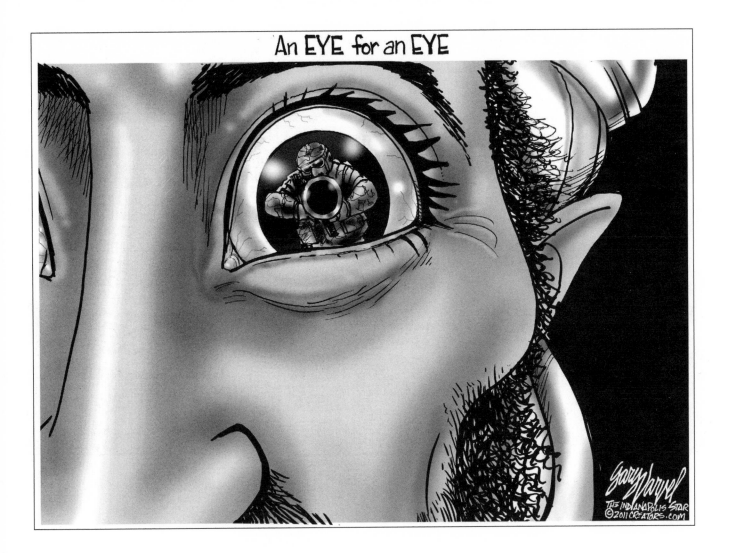

GARY VARVEL

Editorial Cartoonist
Indianapolis Star

Born in Indianapolis, Indiana, 1957; artist for the *Indianapolis News,*
1978-84, and the *Indianapolis Star,* 1984 to the present; nine-time
winner of the Indiana Society of Professional Journalists Award; eight-
time winner of Best Editorial Cartoonist in the Hoosier State Press
Association Competition; motivational speaker; cartoons distributed by
Creators Syndicate.

JACK OHMAN

Editorial Cartoonist
The Oregonian

Born in St. Paul, Minnesota, 1960; graduated with honors from Portland State University; editorial cartoonist for the *Columbus Dispatch,* 1981-82, the *Detroit Free Press,* 1982-83, and *The Oregonian,* 1983 to the present; winner of the Society of Professional Journalists Mark of Excellence Award, 1980, the Thomas Nast Award, 1995, the National Headliner Award, 2002, and the Robert F. Kennedy Journalism Award, 2009; cartoons syndicated by Tribune Media Services.

BEST
EDITORIAL
CARTOONS
OF THE YEAR

MIKE KEEFE
Courtesy Denver Post

JERRY HOLBERT
Courtesy Boston Herald

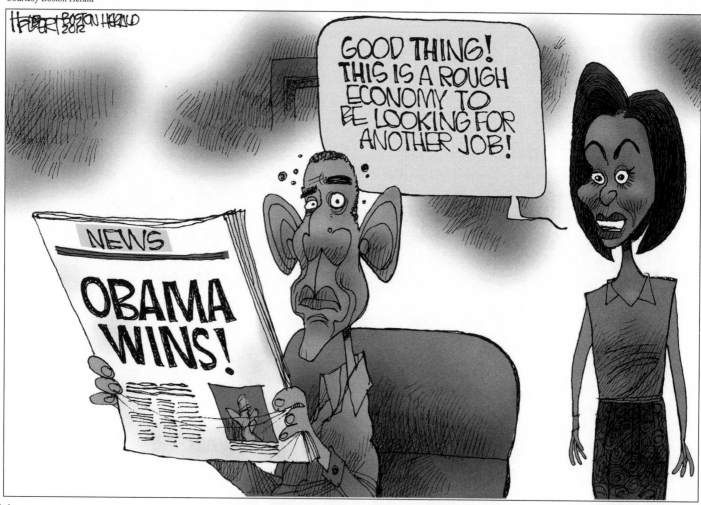

The Winner

President Barack Obama withstood a strong October rally by Republican challenger Mitt Romney to win re-election November 6 to four more years in the White House. Women, Latinos, and the young turned out in large numbers and provided Obama's margin of victory.

It was a come-from-behind victory of sorts. Obama's standing in the polls had plummeted for a time in early October after his poor performance in the first of three televised debates. The president was roundly criticized, even by members of his own party, for what was generally seen as a lackluster effort. He recouped his standing somewhat in the final two debates.

The major issues centered around jobs, a four-year-old recession, and the Obama administration's lack of genuine achievements. On election day, the unemployment rate remained stuck at 7.9 percent, slightly higher than when the president took office in 2009. A $16 trillion national debt and a shaky foreign policy added to Obama's campaign challenge.

The destruction caused by Hurricane Sandy along the Eastern Seaboard at the end of October and the president's subsequent response lifted Obama's campaign, and by election day most pollsters gave him a slight edge.

SCOTT STANTIS
Courtesy Chicago Tribune

15

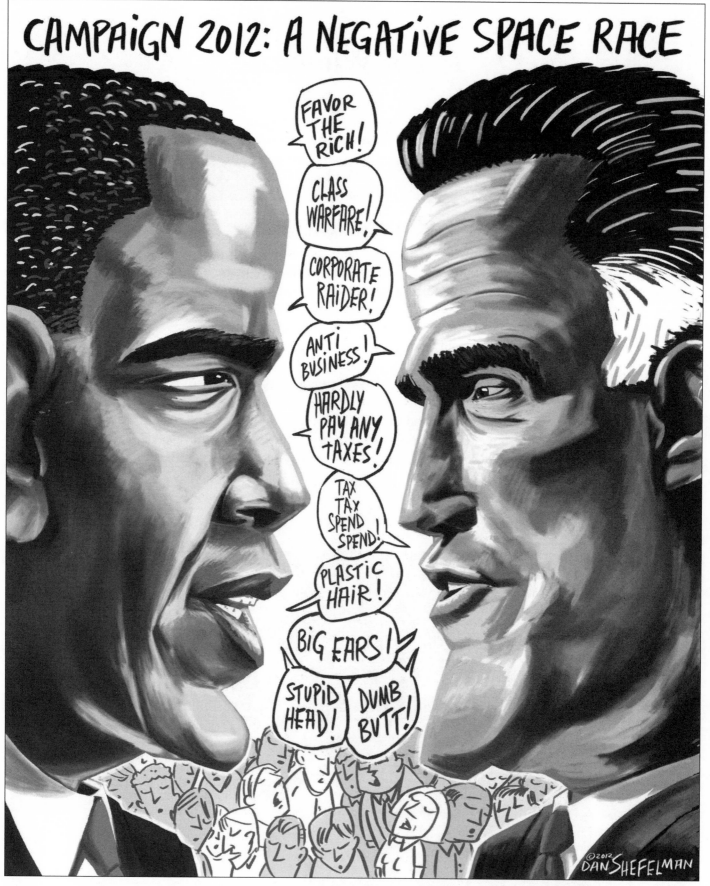

DAN SHEFELMAN
Courtesy Kenyon College Alumni Bulletin

Campaign 2012

The race for the Oval Office featured issues ranging from serious to silly. The sluggish economy threatened to derail President Obama's bid for re-election as unemployment remained around 8 percent and the national debt soared past $16 trillion. Foreign affairs also presented problems for the president's campaign. On the anniversary of the 9/11 terrorist attacks, the American consulate in Benghazi was attacked by terrorists. Ambassador Christopher Stevens and three other Americans were killed.

There was plenty of mudslinging. Senate Majority Leader Harry Reid, citing anonymous sources, claimed that Romney had paid no income taxes for years. The former head of Bain Capital, Romney was portrayed as a wealthy, uncaring businessman. Republican support for voter ID laws was characterized by Democrats as voter suppression.

Republicans seized upon a speech by Obama in which he said that businessmen owed their success to government assistance. The GOP made Obama's "You didn't build that" remark a key theme of its convention. Vice President Joe Biden maintained his propensity for misstatements and outright gaffes.

Romney was criticized for transporting his dog in a carrier on top of his car, and for trying to kill Sesame Street's Big Bird character. Romney's running mate, Rep. Paul Ryan, portrayed himself as a steadfast opponent of government spending.

ROBERT ENGLEHART
Courtesy Hartford Courant

JIMMY MARGULIES
Courtesy The Record (N.J.)

ROB ROGERS
Courtesy Pittsburgh Post-Gazette

ED GAMBLE
Courtesy King Features

JOE HELLER
Courtesy Green Bay Press-Gazette

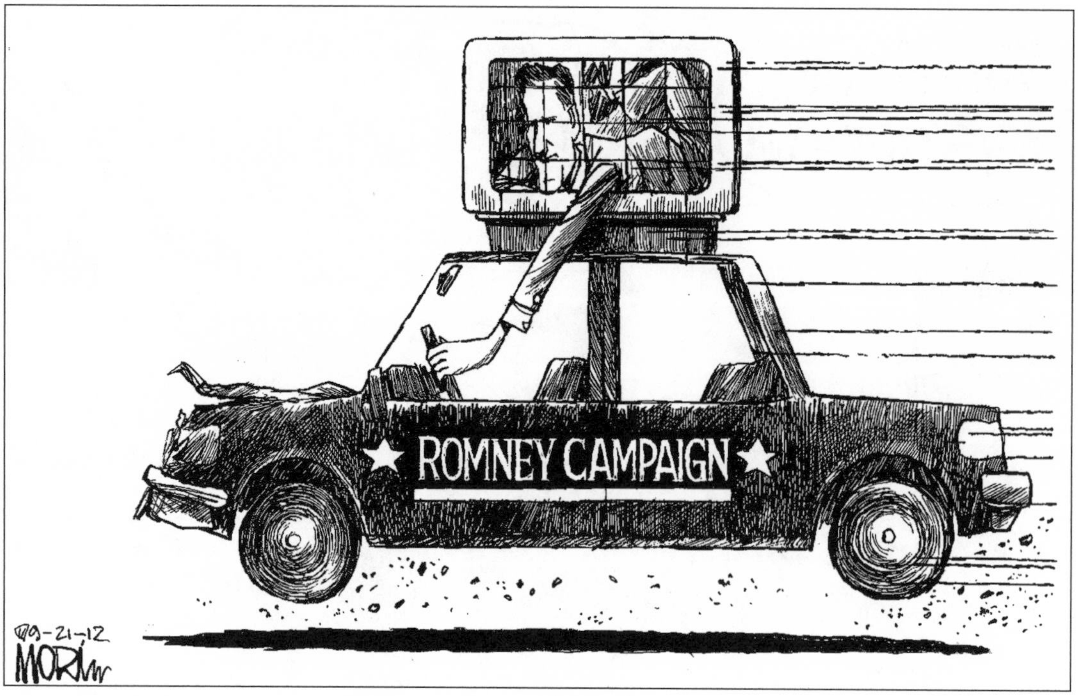
ROMNEY CAMPAIGN
09-21-12
MORIN

JIM MORIN
Courtesy Miami Herald

BRUCE MACKINNON
Courtesy Halifax Chronicle-Herald (N.S.)

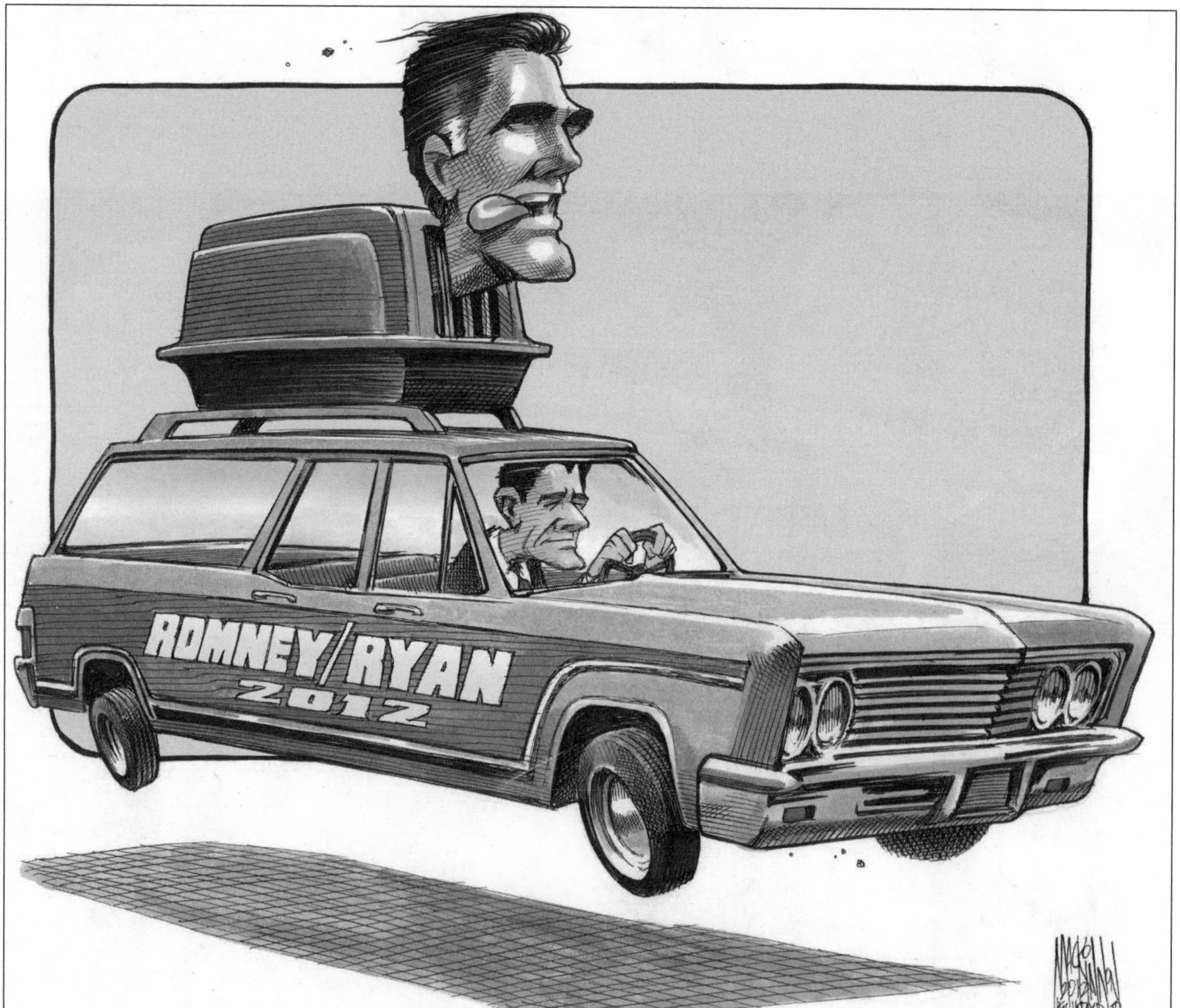
ROMNEY/RYAN
2012

CHIP BOK
Courtesy Creators Syndicate

RICK MCKEE
Courtesy Augusta Chronicle

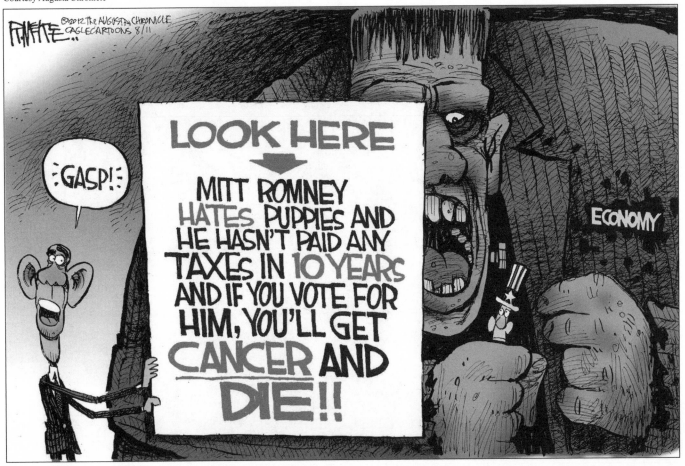

CLAY BENNETT
Courtesy Chattanooga Times-Free Press

JEN SORENSEN
Courtesy Jen Sorensen

'Come on, guys... It's not like I'm trying to vote.'

TAYLOR JONES
Courtesy Cagle Cartoons

PETER DUNLAP-SHOHL
Courtesy Peter Dunlap-Shohl

MATT WUERKER
Courtesy Politico

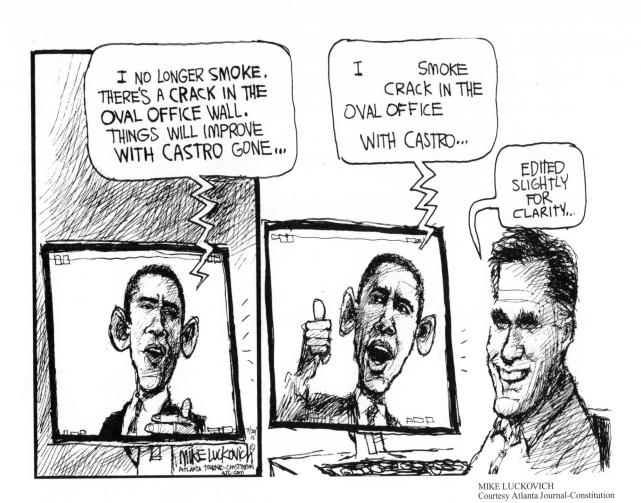

MIKE LUCKOVICH
Courtesy Atlanta Journal-Constitution

TAYLOR JONES
Courtesy Cagle Cartoons

CLAY BENNETT
Courtesy Chattanooga Times-Free Press

ROBERT ARIAIL
Courtesy Spartanburg Herald-Journal

JIM MORIN
Courtesy Miami Herald

CHRIS BRITT
Courtesy State Journal-Register (Ill.)

BOB GORRELL
Courtesy Gorrell Creative

ADAM ZYGLIS
Courtesy Buffalo News

JIM MORIN
Courtesy Miami Herald

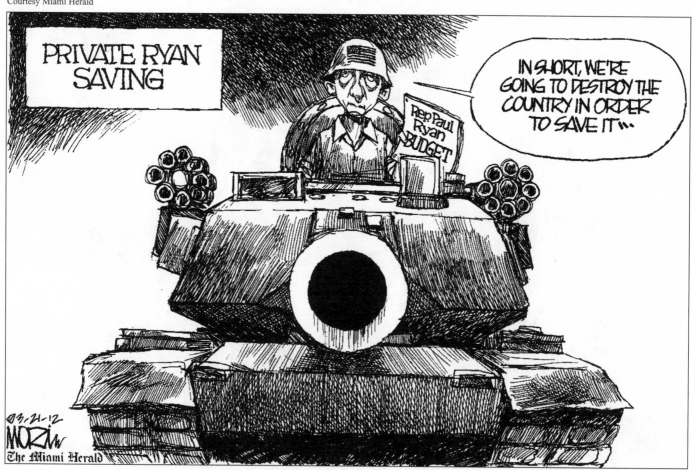

JOE MOHR
Courtesy JoeMohrToons.com

MICHAEL OSBUN
Courtesy Tribune Media Services

MIKE LUCKOVICH
Courtesy Atlanta Journal-Constitution

CLAY BENNETT
Courtesy Chattanooga Times-Free Press

JERRY HOLBERT
Courtesy Boston Herald

STEVE KELLEY
Courtesy The Times-Picayune (La.)

KEVIN KALLAUGHER
Courtesy Baltimore Sun

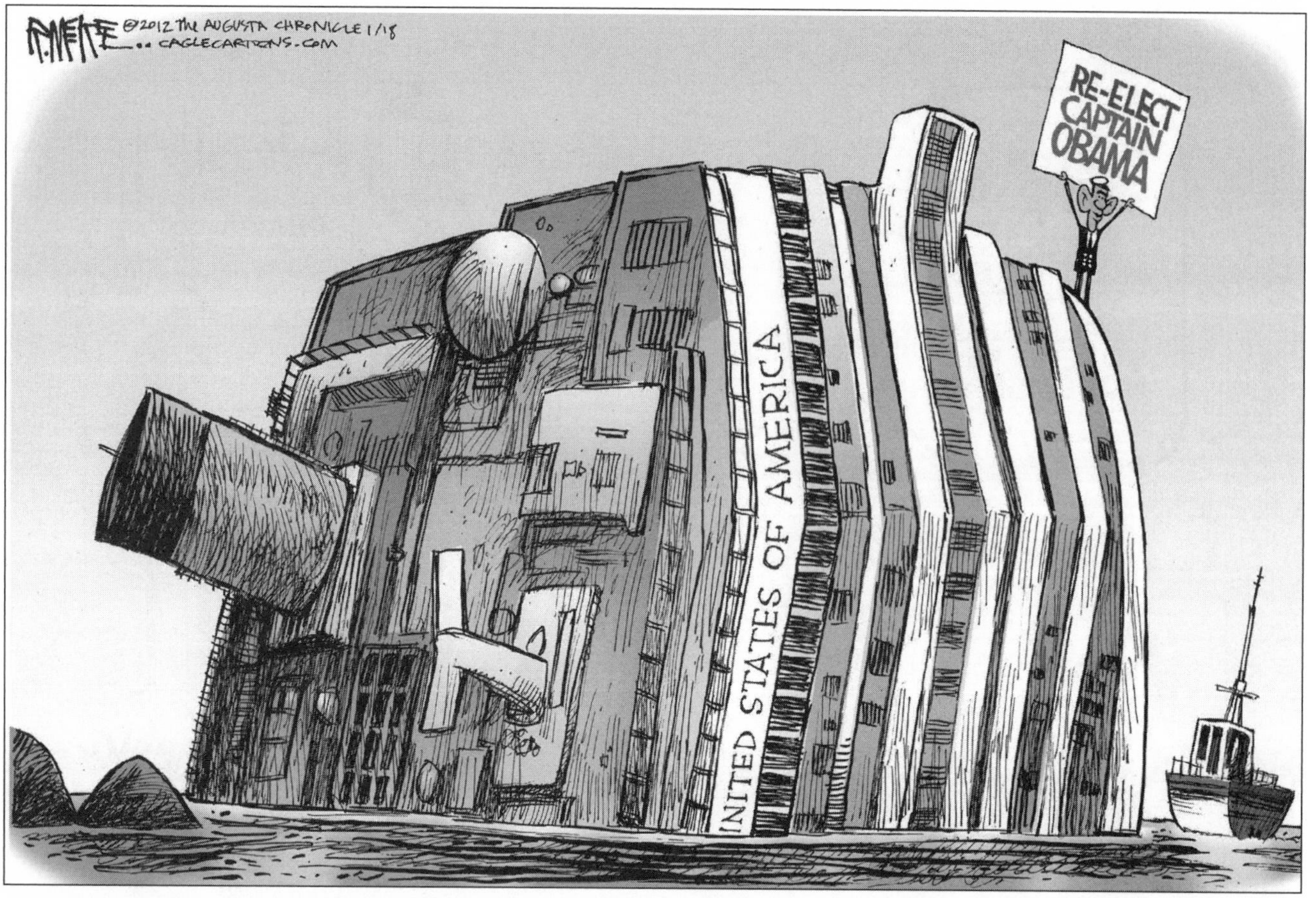
©2012 The Augusta Chronicle 1/18
caglecartoons.com
RE-ELECT CAPTAIN OBAMA
UNITED STATES OF AMERICA

RICK MCKEE
Courtesy Augusta Chronicle

MICHAEL RAMIREZ
Investor's Business Daily

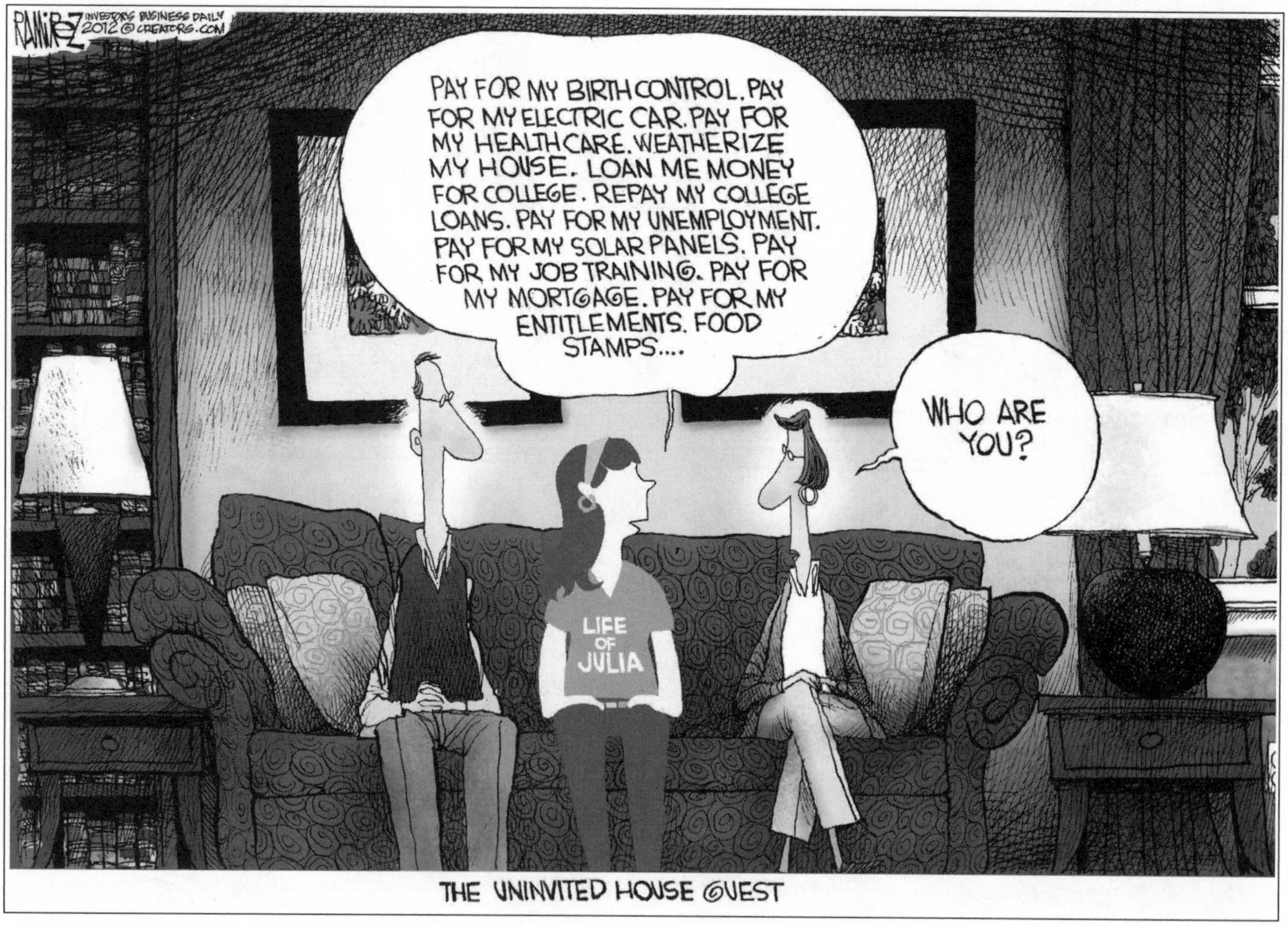
RAMIREZ Investors Business Daily 2012 © creators.com
PAY FOR MY BIRTH CONTROL. PAY FOR MY ELECTRIC CAR. PAY FOR MY HEALTH CARE. WEATHERIZE MY HOUSE. LOAN ME MONEY FOR COLLEGE. REPAY MY COLLEGE LOANS. PAY FOR MY UNEMPLOYMENT. PAY FOR MY SOLAR PANELS. PAY FOR MY JOB TRAINING. PAY FOR MY MORTGAGE. PAY FOR MY ENTITLEMENTS. FOOD STAMPS....
WHO ARE YOU?
LIFE OF JULIA
THE UNINVITED HOUSE GUEST

STEVE KELLEY
Courtesy The Times-Picayune (La.)

JACK OHMAN
Courtesy The Oregonian

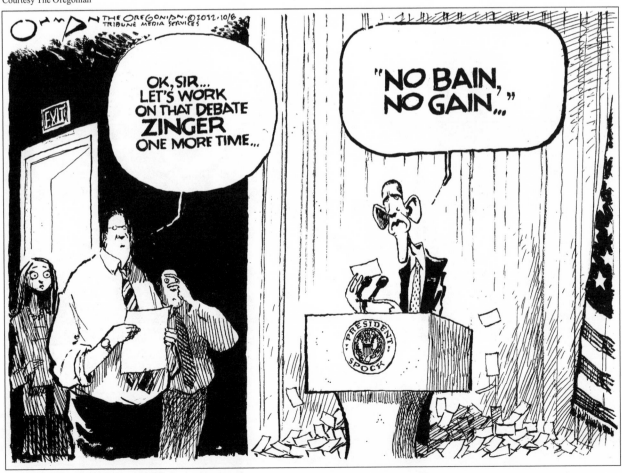

TIM BENSON
Courtesy The Argus-Leader (S.D.)

Conventions and Primaries

Vigorous competition among GOP presidential hopefuls led to a series of televised primary debates. Consistent themes during the Republican primaries were opposition to Obama's health care reform law and the national debt, which skyrocketed to more than $16 trillion.

One by one, candidates dropped from the GOP race. Herman Cain was accused of sexual improprieties. Newt Gingrich was weighed down by political and personal baggage, including divorces. Texas Gov. Rick Perry was embarrassed when, during one of the debates, he forgot one of the three federal departments that he wanted to eliminate. Many thought former Pennsylvania Sen. Rick Santorum was too outspoken about his religious beliefs. Former Massachusetts Gov. Mitt Romney finally won the nomination, despite misgivings from some conservatives. The Republican convention focused on the economy, Obama's health care reform law, and the erosion of individual liberties. Actor Clint Eastwood raised eyebrows at the event when he chatted with an empty chair representing President Obama.

The Democratic convention touted two Obama achievements: saving General Motors and killing Osama bin Laden. Governor Romney was accused of sheltering his money in Cayman Islands banks. Obama's acceptance speech, which had been scheduled at Bank of America Stadium in Charlotte, was moved to a smaller venue indoors when it became clear that organizers couldn't fill the 80,000-seat facility.

NATE BEELER
Courtesy Columbus Dispatch

TIM EAGAN
Courtesy Tim Eagan

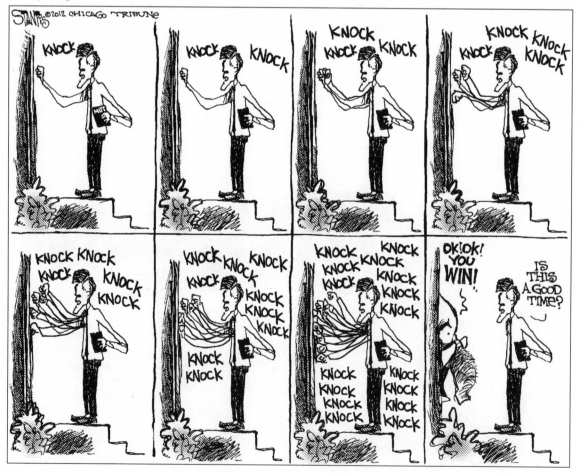

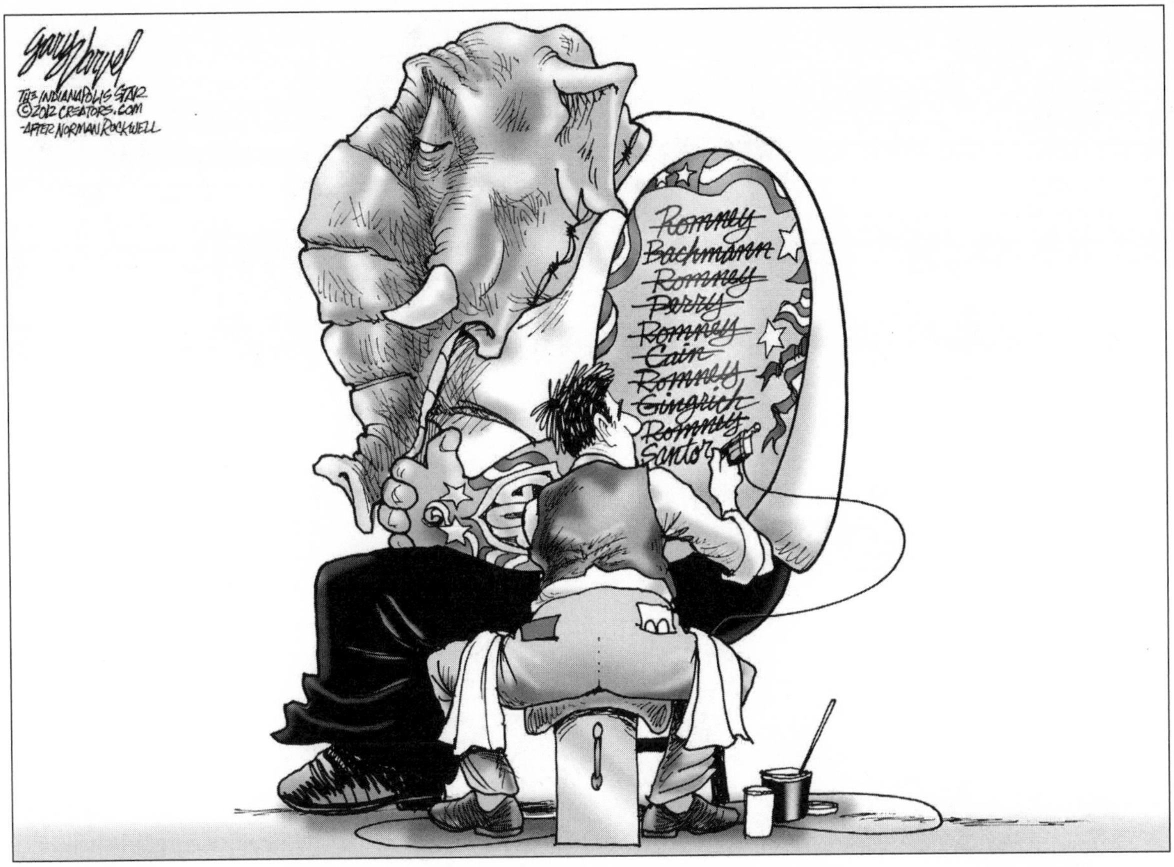

Gary Varvel
THE INDIANAPOLIS STAR
©2012 CREATORS.COM
-AFTER NORMAN ROCKWELL
Romney
Bachmann
Romney
Perry
Romney
Cain
Romney
Gingrich
Romney
Santor

GARY VARVEL
Courtesy Indianapolis Star

CLAY BENNETT
Courtesy Chattanooga Times-Free Press

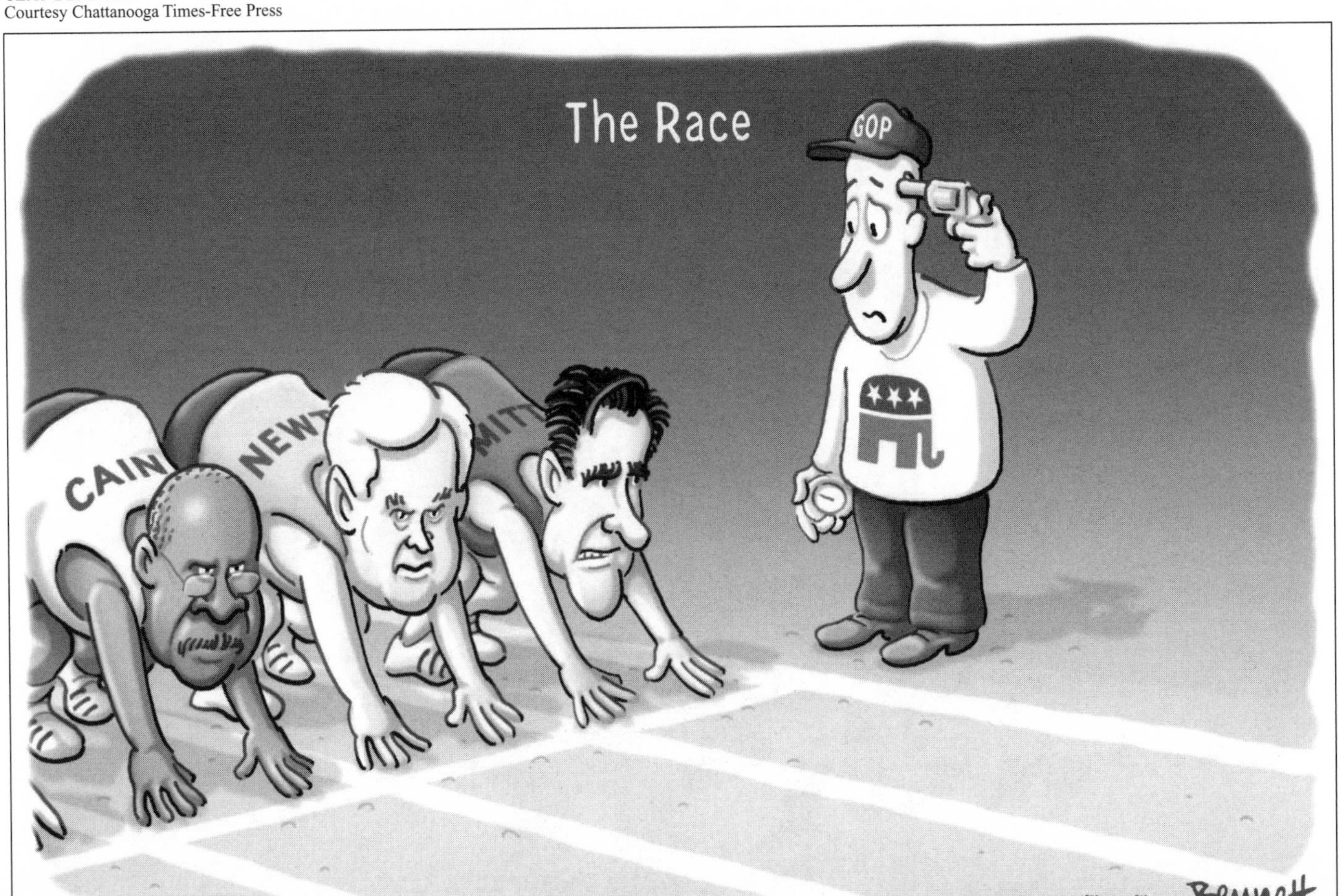

The Race
GOP
CAIN
NEWT
MITT
Chattanooga Times Free Press
Bennett

JERRY HOLBERT
Courtesy Boston Herald

CHRIS BRITT
Courtesy State Journal-Register (Ill.)

MIKE LUCKOVICH
Courtesy Atlanta Journal-Constitution

JOHN TREVER
Courtesy Albuquerque Journal

JACK OHMAN
Courtesy The Oregonian

JIMMY MARGULIES
Courtesy The Record (N.J.)

WALT HANDELSMAN
Courtesy Newsday

JERRY HOLBERT
Courtesy Boston Herald

NATE BEELER
Courtesy Washington Examiner

ROBERT ENGLEHART
Courtesy Hartford Courant

KEVIN KALLAUGHER
Courtesy Baltimore Sun

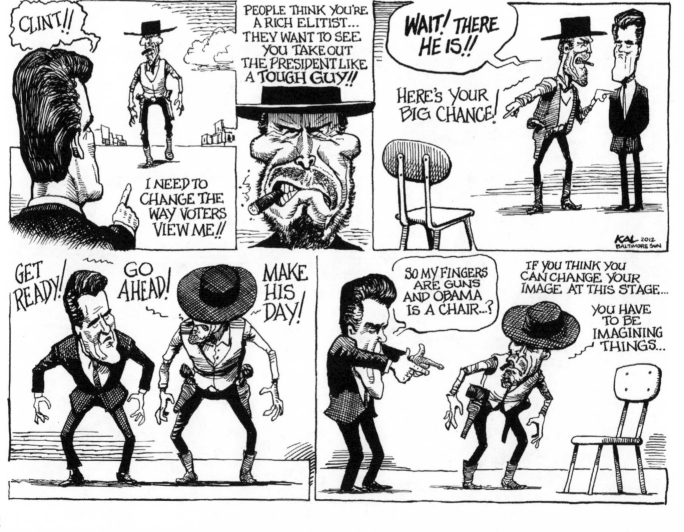

JEFF PARKER
Courtesy Florida Today

DAVID HORSEY
Courtesy Los Angeles Times

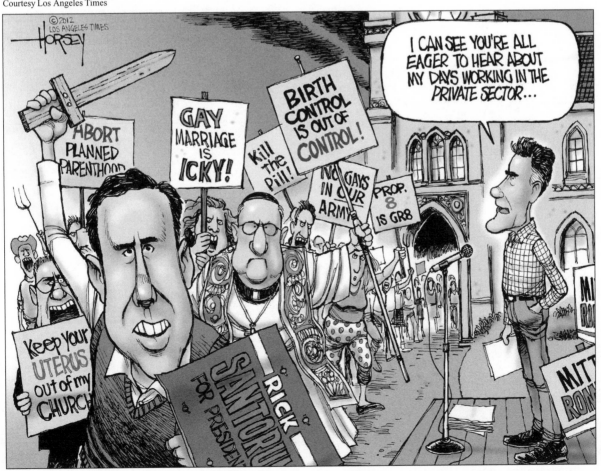

GLENN MCCOY
Courtesy BND Uclick

ED HALL
Courtesy Artizans Syndicate

WALT HANDELSMAN
Courtesy Newsday

44

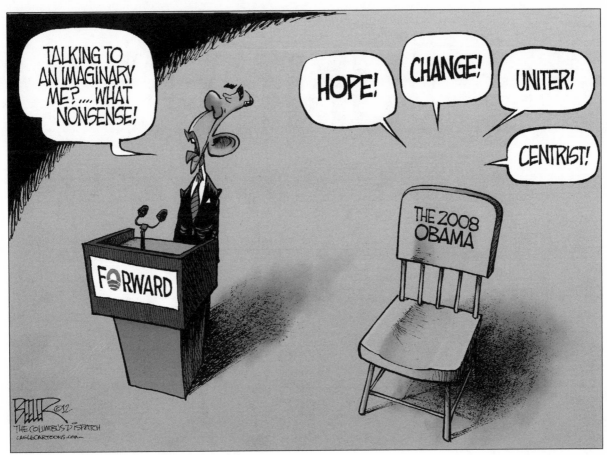

NATE BEELER
Courtesy Columbus Dispatch

JEFFREY DARCY
Courtesy The Plain Dealer (Oh.)

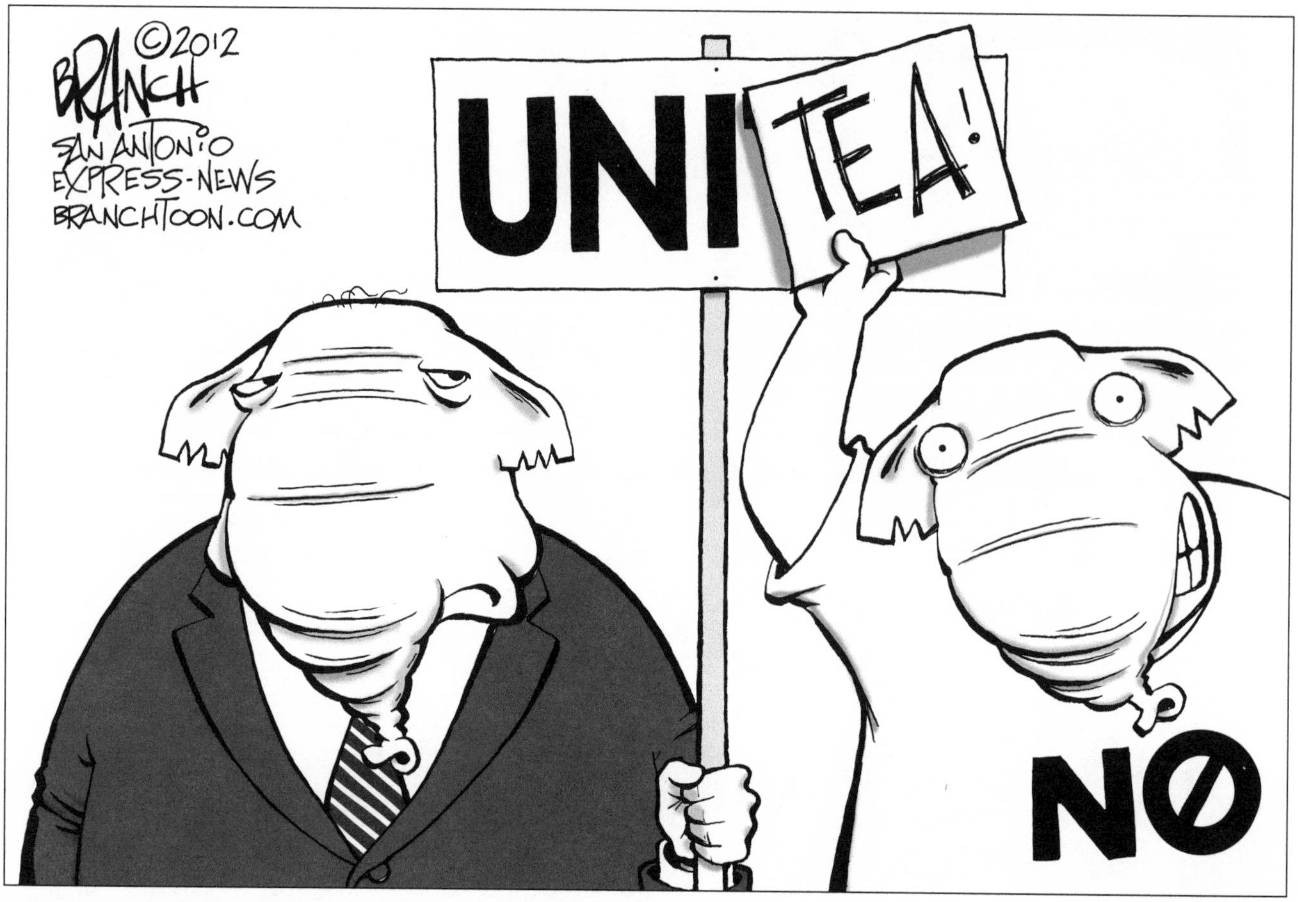

BRANCH ©2012
SAN ANTONIO EXPRESS-NEWS
BRANCHTOON.COM
UNI TEA!
NO

JOHN BRANCH
Courtesy BranchToon.com

RICK MCKEE
Courtesy Augusta Chronicle

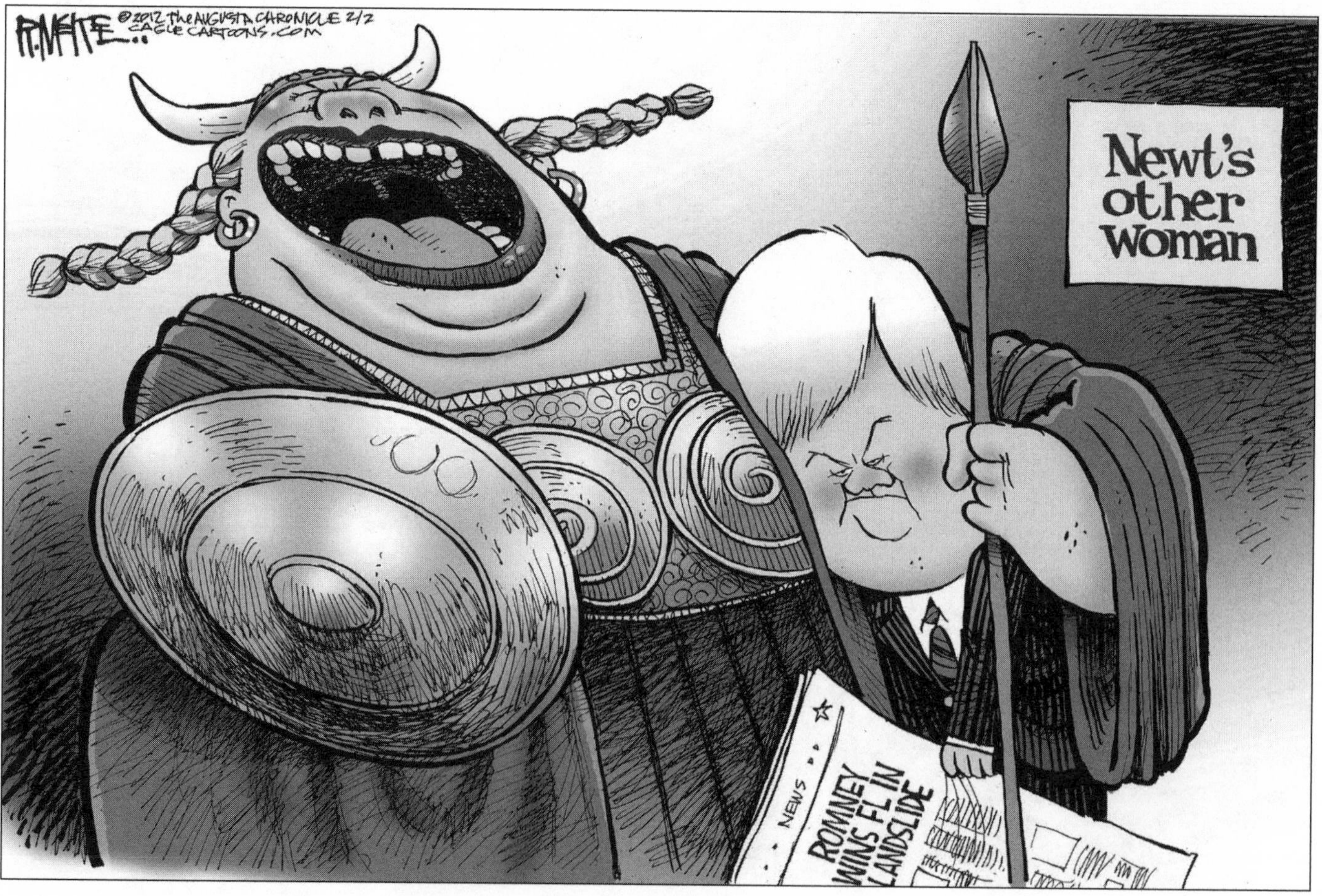

R.MCKEE ©2012 The Augusta Chronicle 2/2
cagle cartoons.com
Newt's other woman
NEWS
ROMNEY WINS FL IN LANDSLIDE

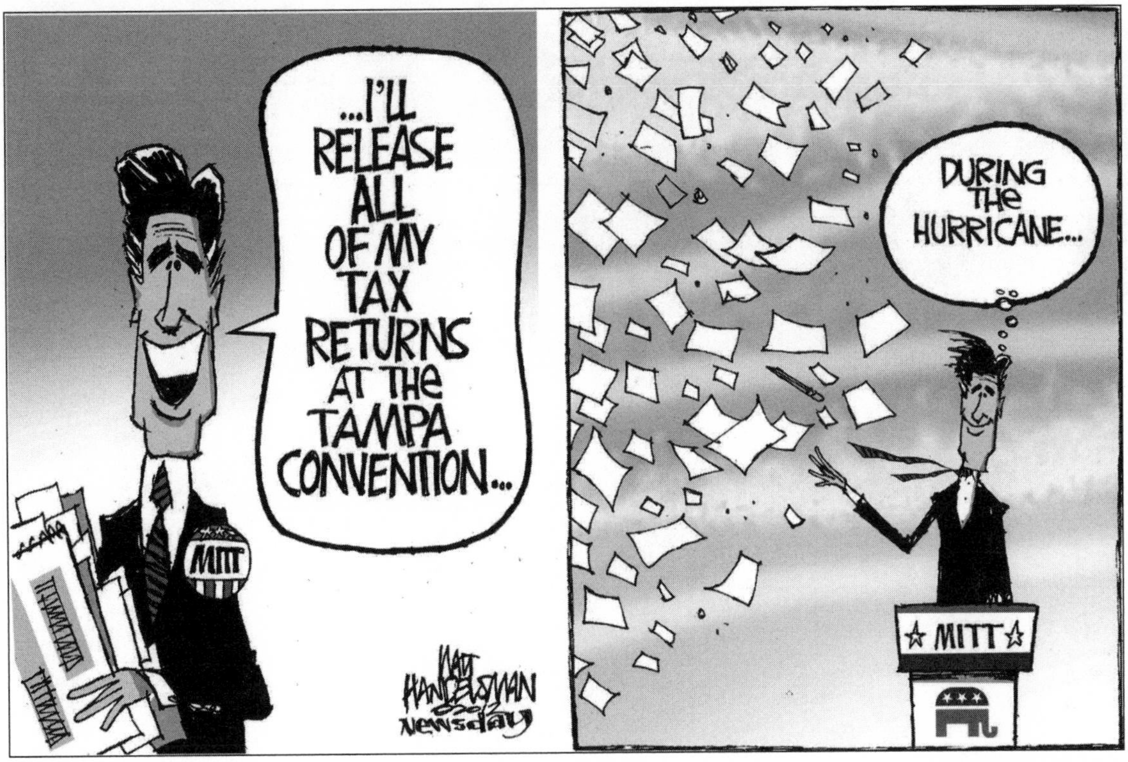
...I'LL RELEASE ALL OF MY TAX RETURNS AT THE TAMPA CONVENTION...
MITT
DURING THE HURRICANE...
MITT
WALT HANDELSMAN
Newsday

WALT HANDELSMAN
Courtesy Newsday

MATT WUERKER
Courtesy Politico

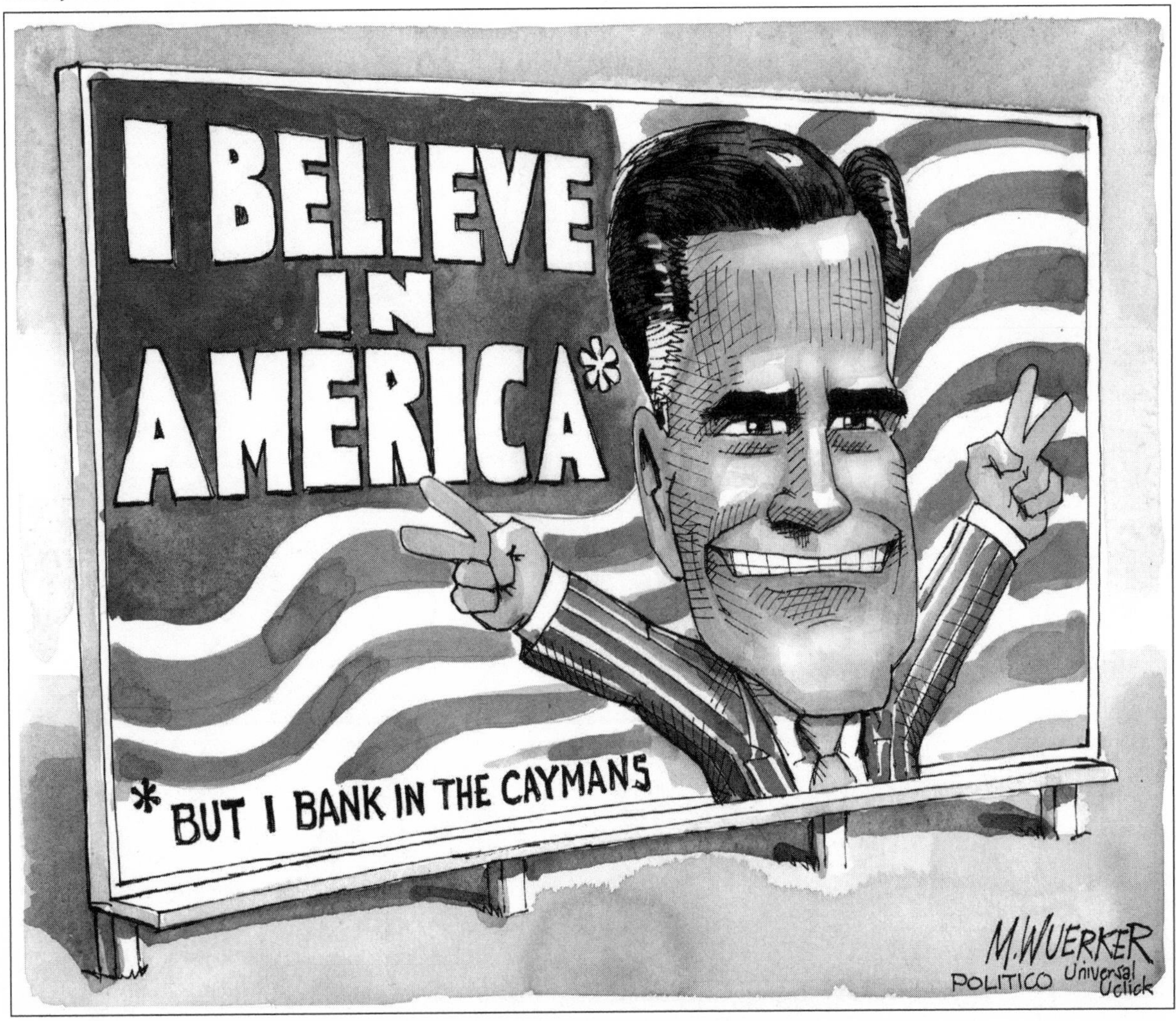
I BELIEVE IN AMERICA*
* BUT I BANK IN THE CAYMANS
M.WUERKER
POLITICO Universal Uclick

GARY MARKSTEIN
Courtesy Creators Syndicate

SCOTT STANTIS
Courtesy Chicago Tribune

BOB GORRELL
Courtesy Gorrell Creative

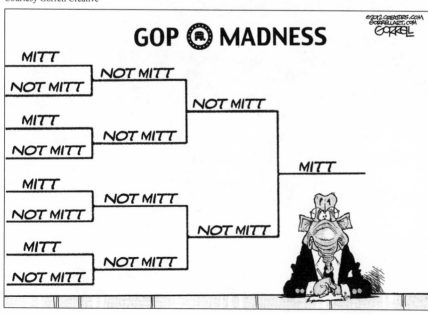

WALT HANDELSMAN
Courtesy Newsday

JEFF PARKER
Courtesy Florida Today

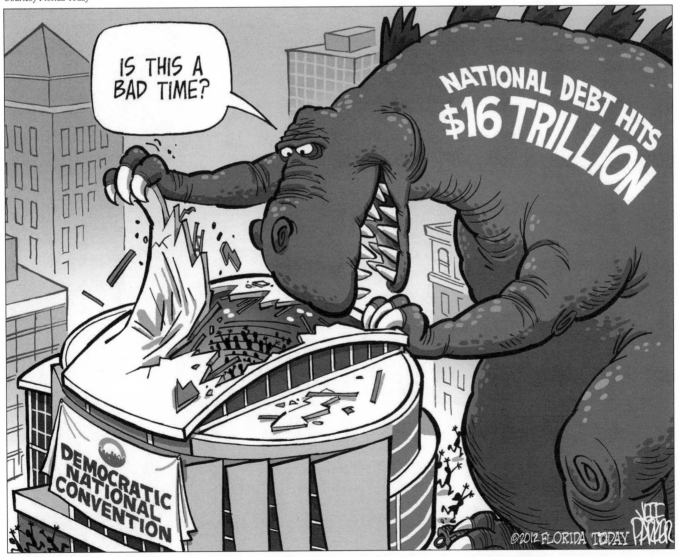

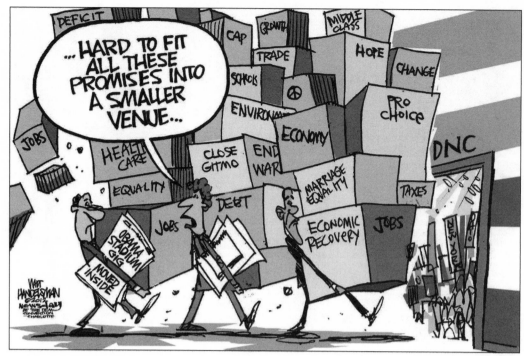

WALT HANDELSMAN
Courtesy Newsday

NICK ANDERSON
Courtesy Houston Chronicle

PHIL HANDS
Courtesy Wisconsin State Journal

51

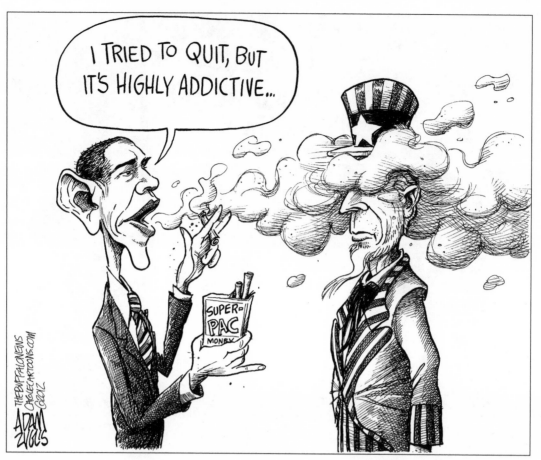

JACK OHMAN
Courtesy The Oregonian

ADAM ZYGLIS
Courtesy Buffalo News

Campaign Finance / Super PACs

Record amounts of money flowed into the 2012 presidential campaign, leading to charges of attempts to buy the election. For the first time ever, one candidate, Barack Obama, raised more than a billion dollars. In September alone, Obama's campaign took in $181 million. Some of the money allegedly came from illegal online donations from foreign countries, according to the conservative Government Accountability Institute. The Obama campaign denied the charge.

Super PACs emerged as a major force in the campaign. The *Wall Street Journal* reported in October that $303,658,213 had been spent on the campaign to that point. Many of the ads were negative, since Super PACs are not held accountable for content. Many Super PAC ads were labeled misleading, such as one questioning Obama's handling of the sacking of the American consulate in Benghazi and ads attacking Romney's stand on abortion. Super PACs are independent political committees that support a candidate with unlimited, often anonymous, donations from companies, unions, or individuals. Super PACs can't contribute directly to a candidate, but they can run favorable—or unfavorable—ads about a candidate.

President Obama was an early critic of the 2010 Supreme Court ruling allowing Super PACs to operate, fearing that corporations would flood the media with support for Republicans. However, Democrats have also benefited from the new source of campaign money.

WALT HANDELSMAN
Courtesy Newsday

JOEL PETT
Courtesy Lexington Herald-Leader

MIKE MARLAND
Courtesy Marland Cartoons

CHRIS BRITT
Courtesy State Journal-Register (Ill.)

54

MATT WUERKER
Courtesy Politico

MATT WUERKER
Courtesy Politico

LISA BENSON
Courtesy Washington Post Writers Group

PAUL FELL
Courtesy Artizans Syndicate

JIM MORIN
Courtesy Miami Herald

The Obama Administration

With the economy struggling, President Obama faced a wide range of criticisms and challenges. He was widely seen as being anti-business. After a speech in which he said that the rich owed at least part of their success to government, his assertion that "you didn't build that" became a rallying cry for Republicans. He was accused of being out of touch when he insisted that the struggling private sector of the economy was "doing fine." His continued opposition to the Keystone pipeline, which would bring Canadian oil to the U.S. and create thousands of jobs, further cemented criticism that the president's policies were damaging the economy.

Sensitive, classified information about the war on terror was leaked, apparently by the White House. With the Mideast aflame, the president turned down a request to meet with Israeli Prime Minister Benjamin Netanyahu. Republicans pointed out that he somehow had made time for fundraisers, golf, and an appearance on the television show "The View." The Justice Department's internal investigation of the gun-walking scheme Fast and Furious faulted the agency for misguided strategies, errors in judgment, and management failures.

President Obama bought a home brewing kit and produced White House Honey Brown Ale. It was thought to be the first alcohol brewed or distilled on White House grounds. Gaffe-prone Vice President Joe Biden told a largely black audience that Governor Romney wants "to put y'all back in chains."

GARY VARVEL
Courtesy Indianapolis Star

57

LISA BENSON
Courtesy Washington Post Writers Group

KEVIN KALLAUGHER
Courtesy Baltimore Sun

GLENN MCCOY
Courtesy BND Uclick

MICHAEL RAMIREZ
Investor's Business Daily

THE DIVERSION

MR. BIDEN, THERE'S A GENTLEMAN HERE WHO WOULD LIKE TO DISCUSS YOUR REMARKS ABOUT REPUBLICANS WANTING TO PUT PEOPLE "BACK IN CHAINS"

RANDY BISH
Courtesy Pittsburgh Tribune-Review

JIM MORIN
Courtesy Miami Herald

GLENN MCCOY
Courtesy BND Uclick

GARY VARVEL
Courtesy Indianapolis Star

61

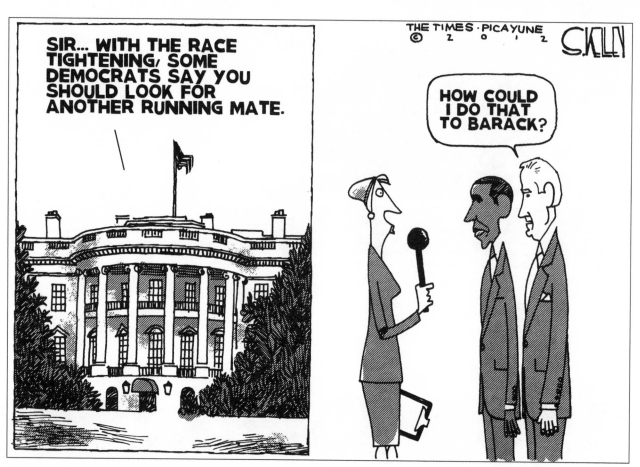

STEVE KELLEY
Courtesy The Times-Picayune (La.)

TOM STIGLICH
Courtesy Northeast Times

GLENN MCCOY
Courtesy BND Uclick

MICHAEL RAMIREZ
Investor's Business Daily

GUY BADEAUX
Courtesy LeDroit (Ottawa)

STEVE BREEN
Courtesy San Diego Union-Tribune

JOHN R. ROSE
Courtesy Byrd Newspapers of Virginia

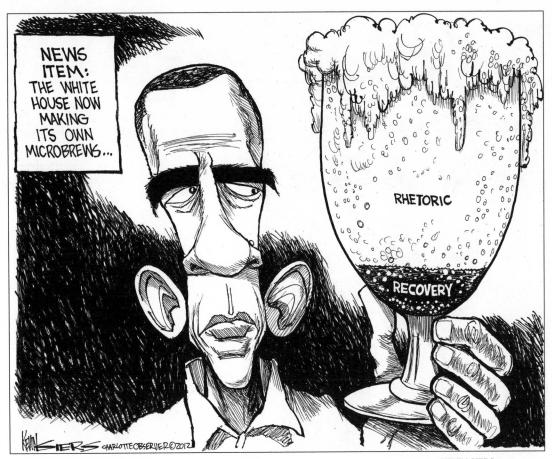

KEVIN SIERS
Courtesy Charlotte Observer

JOHN TREVER
Courtesy Albuquerque Journal

65

GLENN MCCOY
Courtesy BND Uclick

GUS RODRIGUEZ
Courtesy garrinchatoons.com

GLENN FODEN
Courtesy King Features

GLENN MCCOY
Courtesy BND Uclick

67

CHIP BOK
Courtesy Creators Syndicate

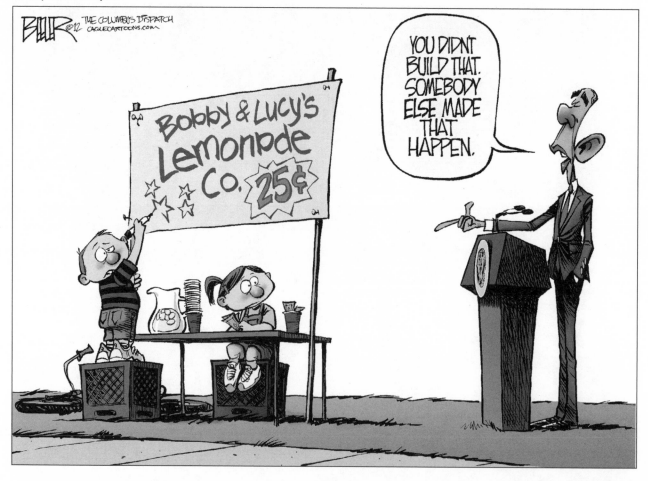

RICK MCKEE
Courtesy Augusta Chronicle

MICHAEL RAMIREZ
Investor's Business Daily

JOHN COLE
Courtesy The Times-Tribune (Pa.)

BOB GORRELL
Courtesy Gorrell Creative

Obamacare

In a major victory for President Obama, the U.S. Supreme Court upheld his signature achievement, the Affordable Health Care Act, also known as Obamacare, in a 5-4 decision. One-time conservative Chief Justice John Roberts cast the deciding vote. In siding with the four liberal justices, Roberts was forced to perform some remarkable legalistic contortions. In order to rule on the law, Roberts said it was not a tax (the court cannot rule on the constitutionality of a tax until it is paid, and Obamacare will not fully go into effect until 2014).

Moreover, Roberts said that the individual mandate, requiring everyone to purchase health insurance, was not justified under the commerce clause of the U.S. Constitution. However, Roberts then declared that the law could be deemed constitutional under Congress' authority to levy taxes. In effect, the law was a tax, and yet was not a tax. GOP presidential candidates, including nominee Mitt Romney, vowed to make the repeal of Obamacare their top priority.

Catholic bishops complained that the Obama administration was forcing religious organizations to provide birth control for employees, although contraception is against church beliefs. Some groups welcomed a compromise offered by the administration, but the bishops maintained that even individual Catholics who own businesses should not be required to provide contraceptives for employees as part of their health insurance coverage.

JOE HELLER
Courtesy Green Bay Press-Gazette

"SIGH... AND JUST WHEN BLAMING ME FOR RUINING THE ECONOMY HAD STOPPED."

STEVE LINDSTROM
Courtesy Duluth News-Tribune

JIMMY MARGULIES
Courtesy The Record (N.J.)

RICHARD LOCHER
Courtesy Tribune Media Services

JIM MORIN
Courtesy Miami Herald

ADAM ZYGLIS
Courtesy Buffalo News

ROBERT ENGLEHART
Courtesy Hartford Courant

KEVIN KALLAUGHER
Courtesy Baltimore Sun

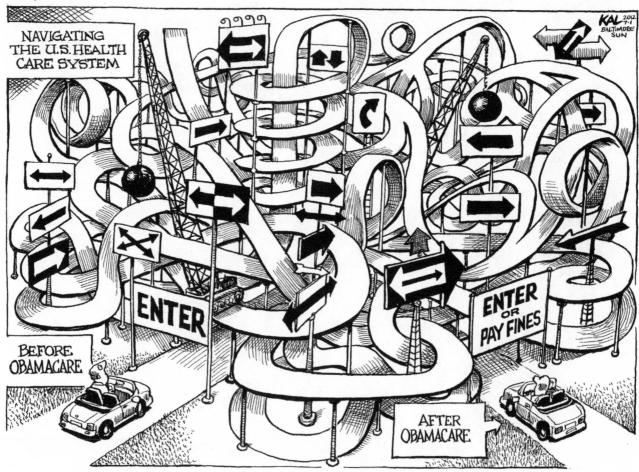

JEFF PARKER
Courtesy Florida Today

ROB ROGERS
Courtesy Pittsburgh Post-Gazette

LISA BENSON
Courtesy Washington Post Writers Group

NATE BEELER
Courtesy Columbus Dispatch

The Economy

The U.S. economy remained in the grip of recession throughout 2012, although some observers reported there were indications of a weak recovery. The unemployment rate held steady at around 8 percent, dipping slightly just weeks before the presidential election. Good-paying jobs with benefits were still being lost, however, as employers, partly to avoid the added cost of Obamacare, hired fewer full-time employees and more part-time workers.

Wages were virtually stagnant. The national debt continued to grow. Graduating seniors found themselves faced with large student loans, limited job prospects, and fierce competition for the few jobs available. Near year's end, the nationwide average price of a gallon of gas had risen to almost four dollars.

Enrollment in federal welfare programs such as food stamps, Medicaid, and disability aid rose much faster than job growth, increasing the culture of dependence on government. Almost 47 million people were receiving food stamps, virtually twice that of four years ago. It is feared by many that unsustainable federal spending could send the U.S. into an economic crisis similar to that facing much of Europe, especially Greece, Italy, and Spain.

The convoluted U.S. tax structure has fostered an exponential growth in lobbyists eager to exploit loopholes for their clients.

TED RALL
Courtesy Universal Uclick

CHIP BOK
Courtesy Creators Syndicate

BRUCE PLANTE
Courtesy Tulsa World

JEFF PARKER
Courtesy Florida Today

JIMMY MARGULIES
Courtesy The Record (N.J.)

79

JERRY HOLBERT
Courtesy Boston Herald

RICHARD LOCHER
Courtesy Tribune Media Services

CHIP BOK
Courtesy Creators Syndicate

MICHAEL RAMIREZ
Investor's Business Daily

JEFF STAHLER
Courtesy GOCOMICS.COM

DEB MILBRATH
Courtesy Deb Milbrath

LARRY WRIGHT
Courtesy Cagle Cartoons

82

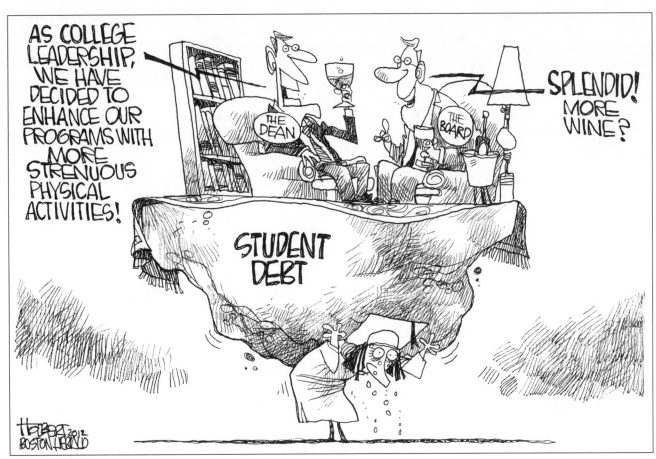

JERRY HOLBERT
Courtesy Boston Herald

RICHARD LOCHER
Courtesy Tribune Media Services

ROBERT ARIAIL
Courtesy Spartanburg Herald-Journal

MILT PRIGGEE
Courtesy Puget Sound Business Journal

JIM DYKE
Courtesy Jefferson City News-Tribune

MIKE LESTER
Courtesy Washington Post Writers Group

WALT HANDELSMAN
Courtesy Newsday

CHRIS BRITT
Courtesy State Journal-Register (Ill.)

STEVE KELLEY
Courtesy The Times-Picayune (La.)

MATT WUERKER
Courtesy Politico

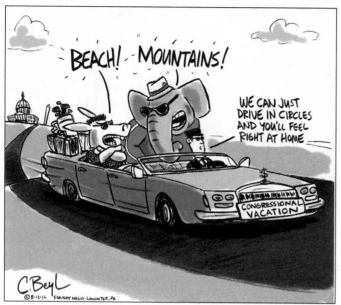

CHARLES BEYL
Courtesy The Sunday News (Pa.)

ROBERT ARIAIL
Courtesy Spartanburg Herald-Journal

STEVE LINDSTROM
Courtesy Duluth News-Tribune

CHIP BOK
Courtesy Creators Syndicate

MICHAEL RAMIREZ
Investor's Business Daily

GARY VARVEL
Courtesy Indianapolis Star

PAUL BERGE
Courtesy Q Syndicate

ROBERT ARIAIL
Courtesy Spartanburg Herald-Journal

GUS RODRIGUEZ
Courtesy garrinchatoons.com

SCOTT STANTIS
Courtesy Chicago Tribune

NICK ANDERSON
Courtesy Houston Chronicle

MATT WUERKER
Courtesy Politico

93

SCOTT STANTIS
Courtesy Chicago Tribune

LISA BENSON
Courtesy Washington Post Writers Group

RANDALL ENOS
Courtesy Cagle Cartoons

JOE HELLER
Courtesy Green Bay Press-Gazette

ERIC SEMELROTH
Courtesy Eric Semelroth

NATE BEELER
Courtesy Washington Examiner

GLENN MCCOY
Courtesy BND Uclick

RICK MCKEE
Courtesy Augusta Chronicle

WALT HANDELSMAN
Courtesy Newsday

WILLIAM FLINT
Courtesy Dallas Morning News

Foreign Affairs

In the evening of the anniversary of the 9/11 terrorist attacks, dozens of heavily armed men stormed the U.S. consulate in Libya, killing Ambassador Christopher Stevens and three other Americans. The Obama administration for days afterward attempted to blame the attack on an obscure anti-Muslim video on YouTube, but later was forced to admit that it was a planned terrorist attack. Obama was accused of apologizing for the video after Americans were killed. The video was also blamed for riots in Egypt, Afghanistan, and other Muslim countries.

The Obama Administration's Arab Spring appeared more and more like an Arab winter. The Middle East teetered on the verge of war. In Syria, tens of thousands of citizens were slaughtered by the Assad regime. Russia continued to supply the tyrant with weapons. The violence spilled over into Turkey when Syria shot down a Turkish warplane and shelled refugees who fled across the border. Turkey responded in kind.

Iran continued its drive to develop nuclear weapons, threatening the existence of Israel. Israeli Prime Minister Benjamin Netanyahu illustrated the threat with a graphic shaped like a bomb. President Obama declined to meet with Netanyahu, further straining U.S.-Israeli relations. American drones continued to target suspected terrorists. Economic woes led to violence in Greece, Spain, and Italy, as citizens protested austerity measures aimed at staving off government bankruptcy.

WAYNE STROOT
Courtesy Hastings Tribune

99

JERRY HOLBERT
Courtesy Boston Herald

GUS RODRIGUEZ
Courtesy garrinchatoons.com

MICHAEL RAMIREZ
Investor's Business Daily

JIM MORIN
Courtesy Miami Herald

JACK OHMAN
Courtesy The Oregonian

THEO MOUDAKIS
Courtesy Toronto Star (Can.)

MIKE PETERS
Courtesy Dayton Daily News

CHIP BOK
Courtesy Creators Syndicate

GUY BADEAUX
Courtesy LeDroit (Ottawa)

STEVE NEASE
Courtesy Nease Cartoons

ROBERT ARIAIL
Courtesy Spartanburg Herald-Journal

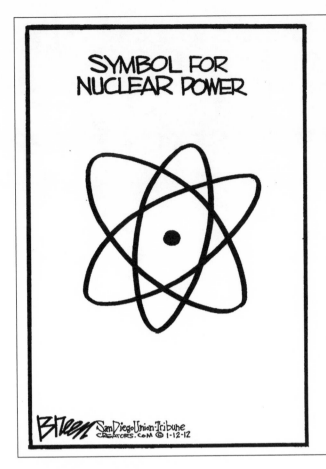

STEVE BREEN
Courtesy San Diego Union-Tribune

ED GAMBLE
Courtesy King Features

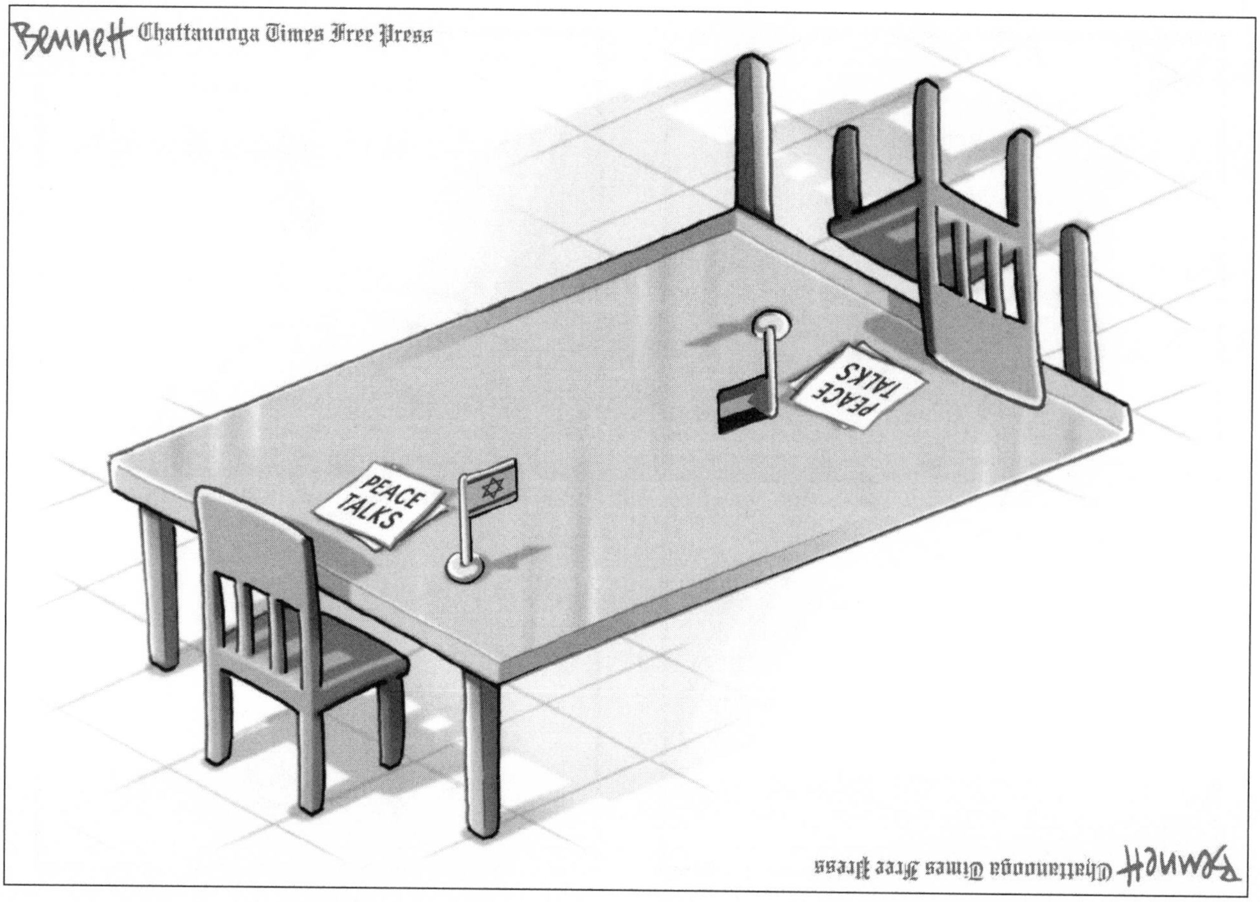
Bennett Chattanooga Times Free Press
PEACE TALKS
PEACE TALKS
Bennett Chattanooga Times Free Press

CLAY BENNETT
Courtesy Chattanooga Times-Free Press

JOEL PETT
Courtesy Lexington Herald-Leader

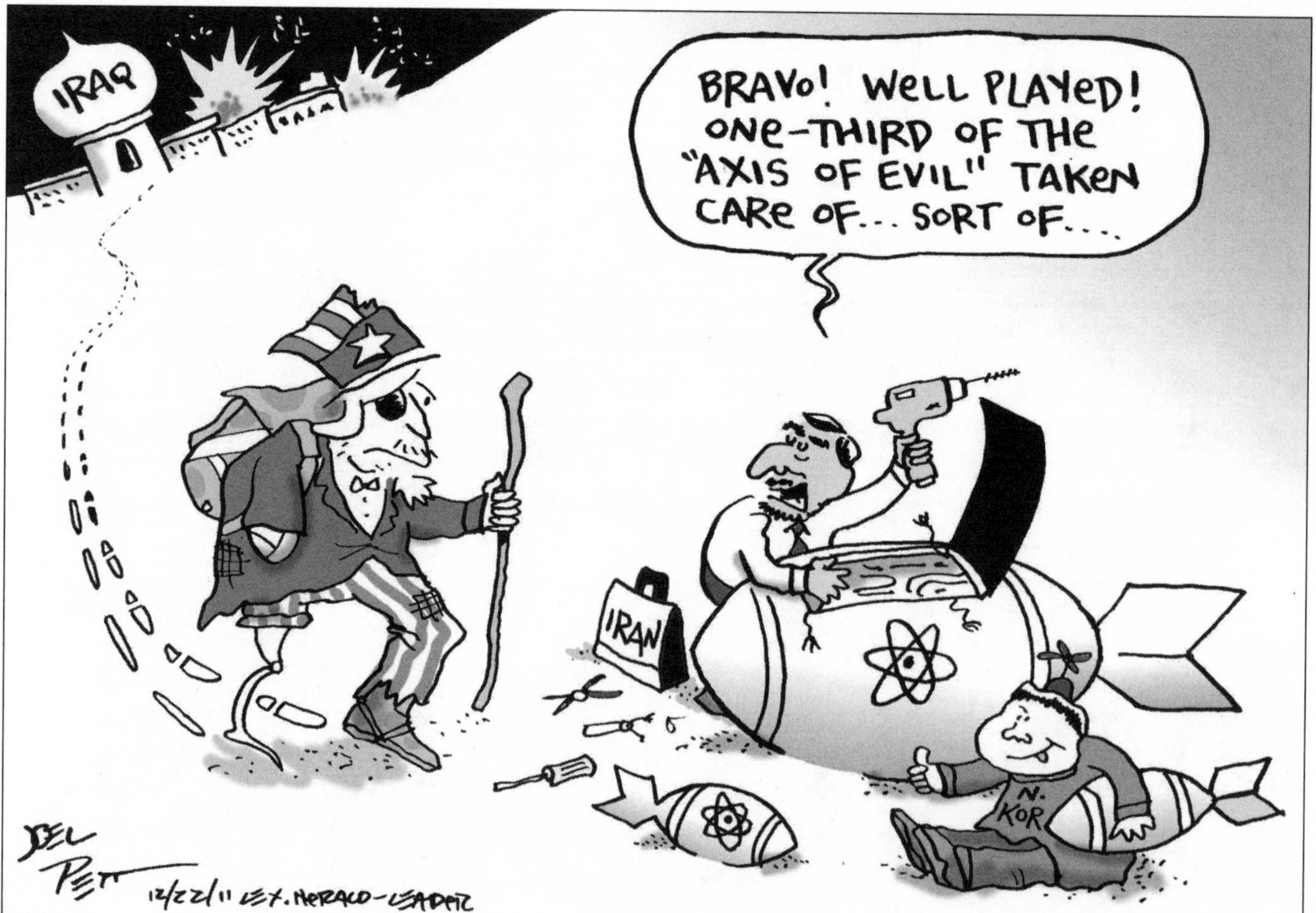
IRAQ
BRAVO! WELL PLAYED! ONE-THIRD OF THE "AXIS OF EVIL" TAKEN CARE OF... SORT OF....
IRAN
N. KOR
JOEL PETT
12/22/11 LEX. HERALD-LEADER

STEVE BREEN
Courtesy San Diego Union-Tribune

TIM BENSON
Courtesy The Argus-Leader (S.D.)

GUS RODRIGUEZ
Courtesy garrinchatoons.com

BOB GORRELL
Courtesy Gorrell Creative

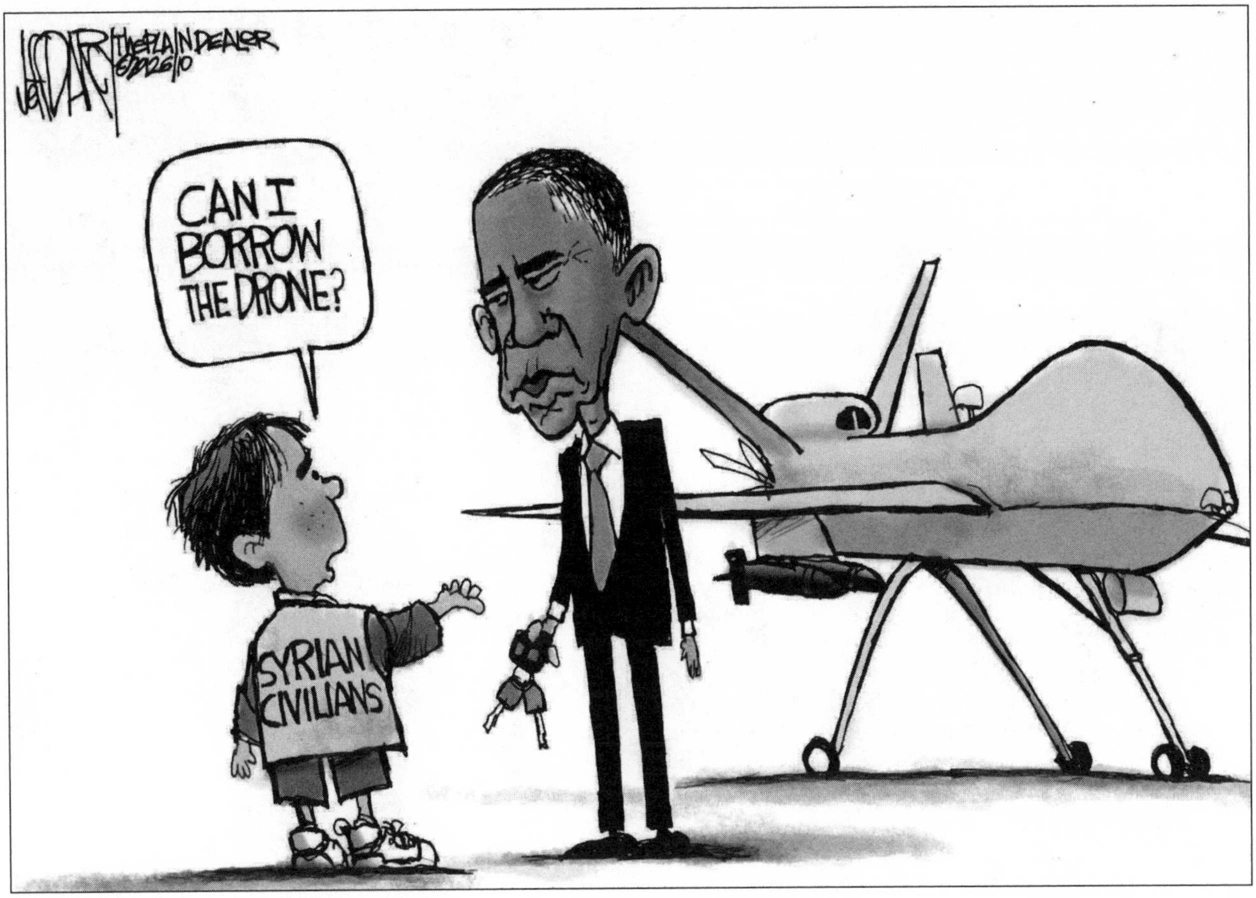
JEFF DARCY THE PLAIN DEALER
CAN I BORROW THE DRONE?
SYRIAN CIVILIANS

JEFFREY DARCY
Courtesy The Plain Dealer (Oh.)

ROB ROGERS
Courtesy Pittsburgh Post-Gazette

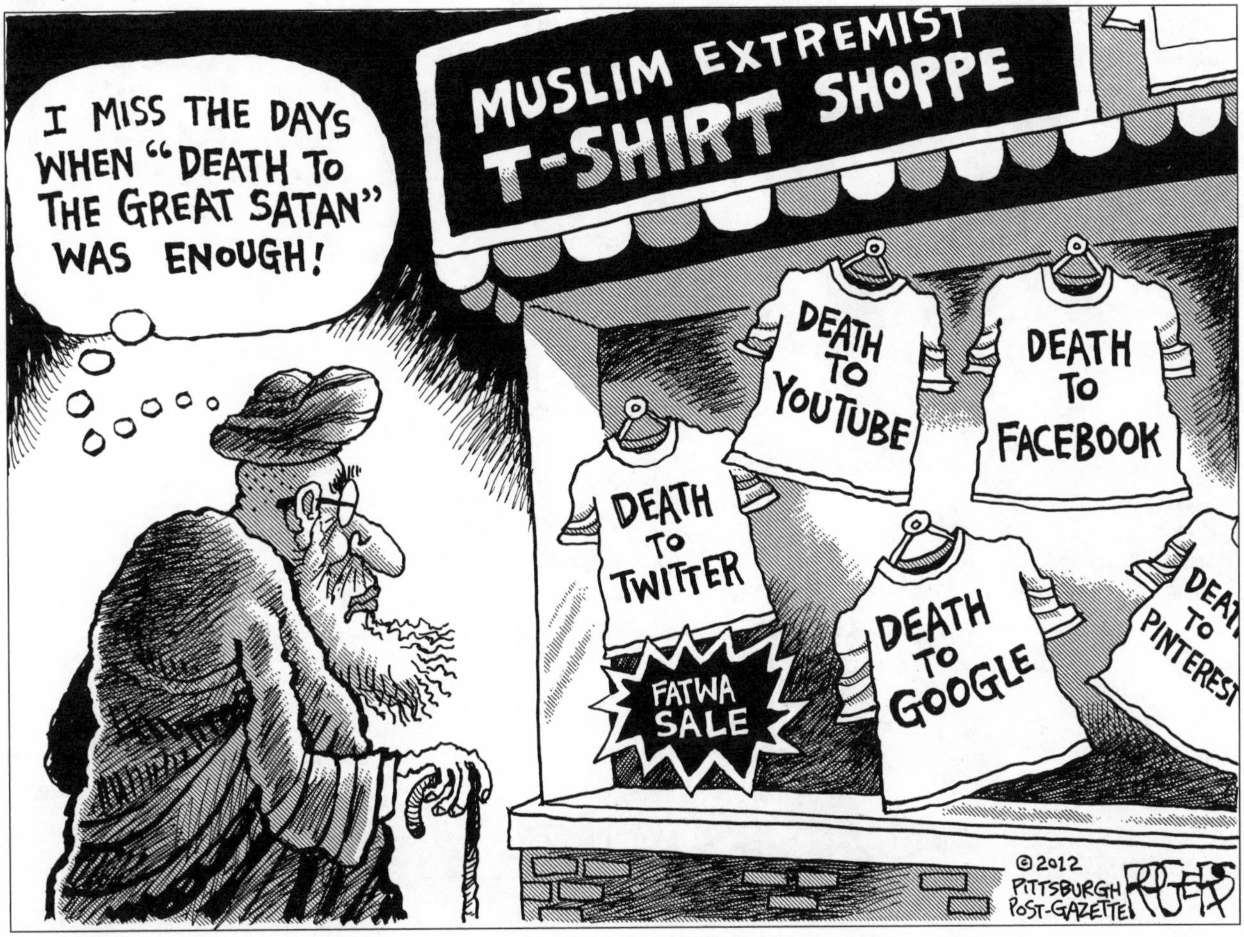
MUSLIM EXTREMIST
T-SHIRT SHOPPE
I MISS THE DAYS WHEN "DEATH TO THE GREAT SATAN" WAS ENOUGH!
DEATH TO YOUTUBE
DEATH TO FACEBOOK
DEATH TO TWITTER
DEATH TO GOOGLE
TO PINTEREST
FATWA SALE
©2012 PITTSBURGH POST-GAZETTE ROGERS

GEORGE DANBY
Courtesy Bangor Daily News

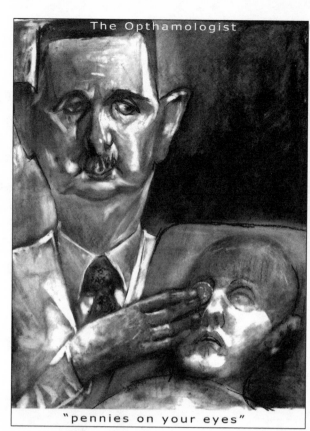

FRED SEBASTIAN
Courtesy Fred Sebastian

JIMMY MARGULIES
Courtesy The Record (N.J.)

MIKE LESTER
Courtesy Washington Post Writers Group

MIKE KEEFE
Courtesy Denver Post

The Arab Street Reacts...

DARYL CAGLE
Courtesy Cagle Cartoons

JEFFREY DARCY
Courtesy The Plain Dealer (Oh.)

CHRIS BRITT
Courtesy State Journal-Register (Ill.)

ROBERT ARIAIL
Courtesy Spartanburg Herald-Journal

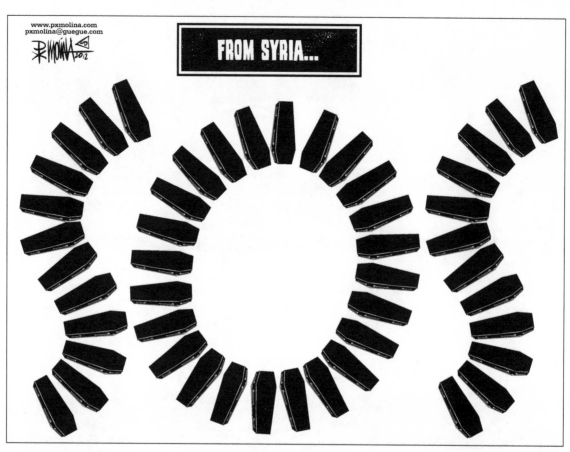

FROM SYRIA...

PEDRO X. MOLINA
Courtesy El Nuevo Diario

TAYLOR JONES
Courtesy Cagle Cartoons

©Taylor Jones - El Nuevo Día

caglecartoons.com

PEDRO X. MOLINA
Courtesy El Nuevo Diario

MIKE KEEFE
Courtesy Denver Post

FRED CURATOLO
Courtesy Fred Curatolo

STEVE LINDSTROM
Courtesy Duluth News-Tribune

STEVE BREEN
Courtesy San Diego Union-Tribune

GARY VARVEL
Courtesy Indianapolis Star

KEVIN KALLAUGHER
Courtesy The Economist

SYRIAL KILLER

BOB GORRELL
Courtesy Gorrell Creative

CHUCK ASAY
Courtesy Creators Syndicate

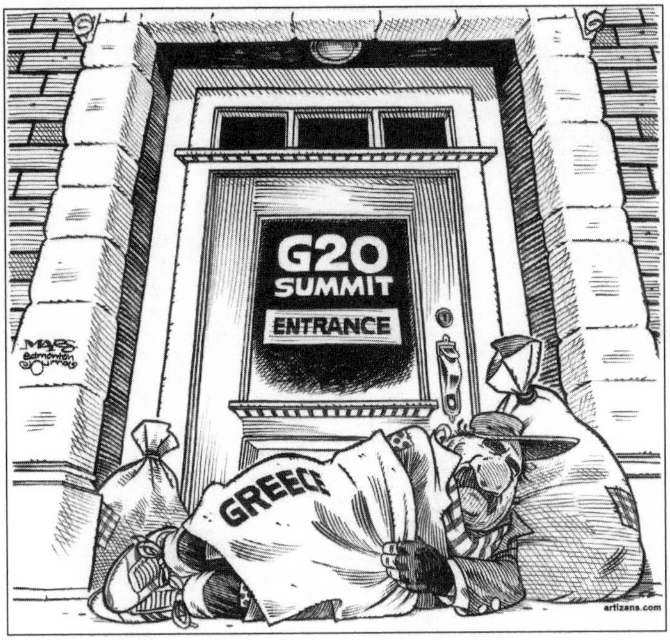
G20
SUMMIT
ENTRANCE
GREECE
artizans.com

MALCOLM MAYES
Courtesy Edmonton Journal (Can.)

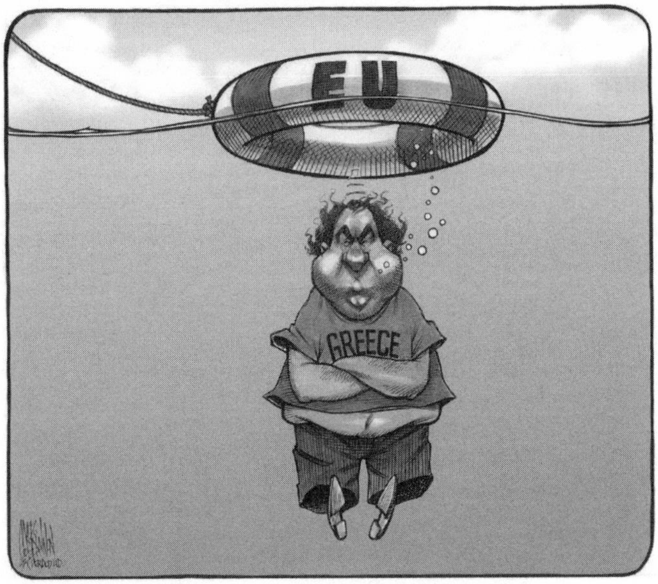
EU
GREECE

BRUCE MACKINNON
Courtesy Halifax Chronicle-Herald (N.S.)

JOHN LARTER
Courtesy Calgary Herald (Can.)

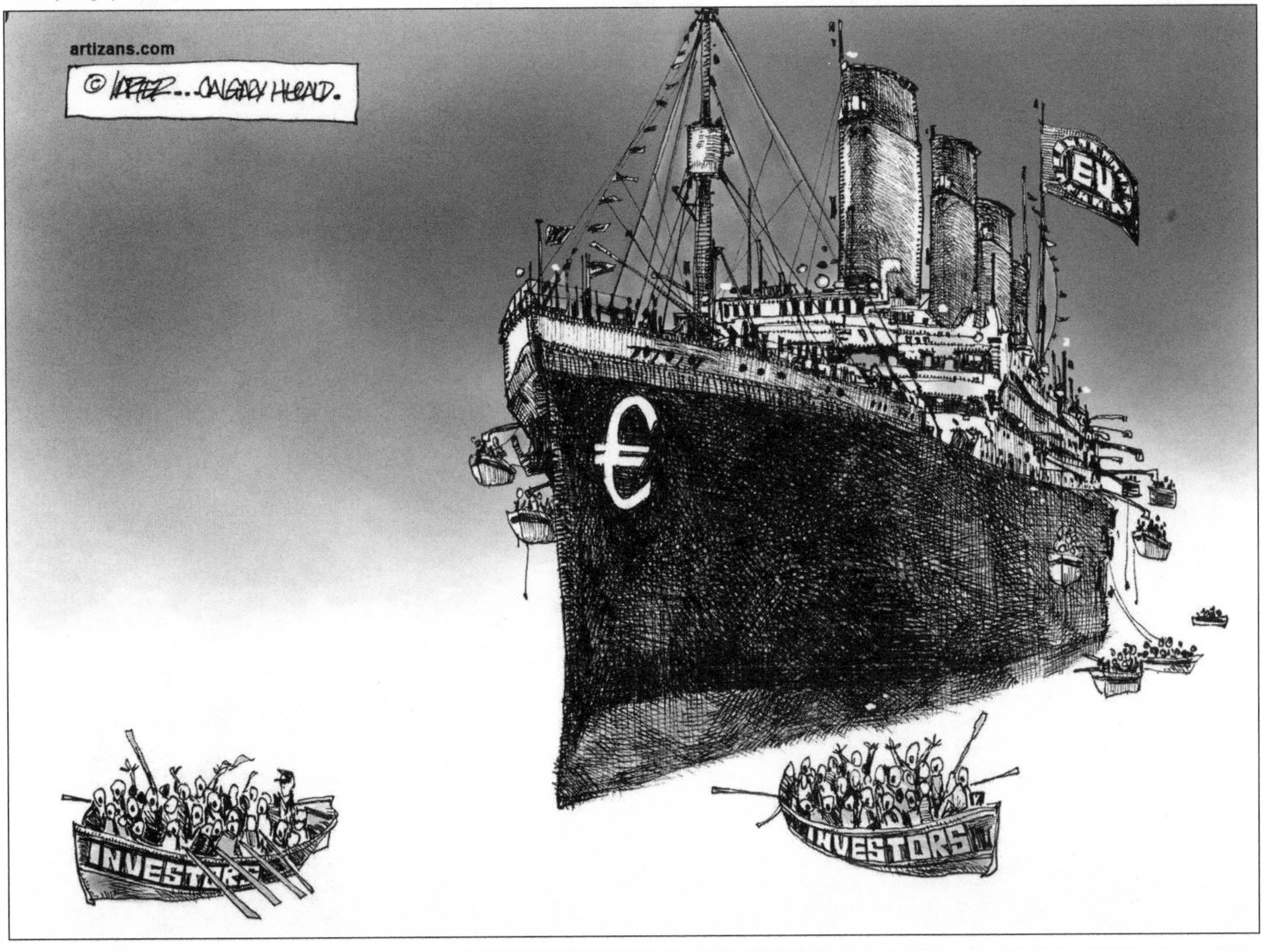
artizans.com
EU
€
INVESTORS
INVESTORS

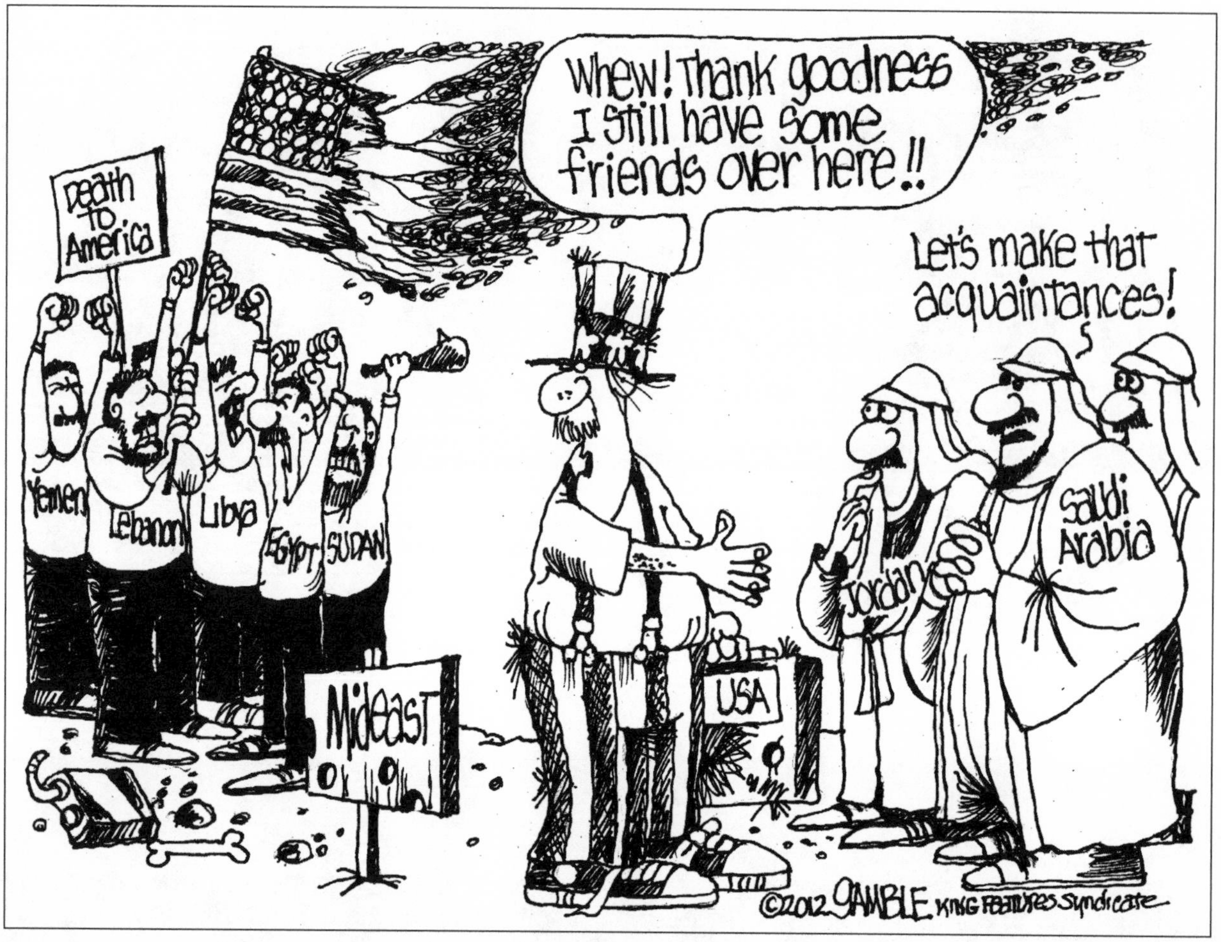
Whew! Thank goodness I still have some friends over here!!
Let's make that acquaintances!
Death to America
Yemen
Lebanon
Libya
EGYPT
SUDAN
Mideast
USA
Jordan
Saudi Arabia
©2012 GAMBLE King Features Syndicate

ED GAMBLE
Courtesy King Features

BOB GORRELL
Courtesy Gorrell Creative

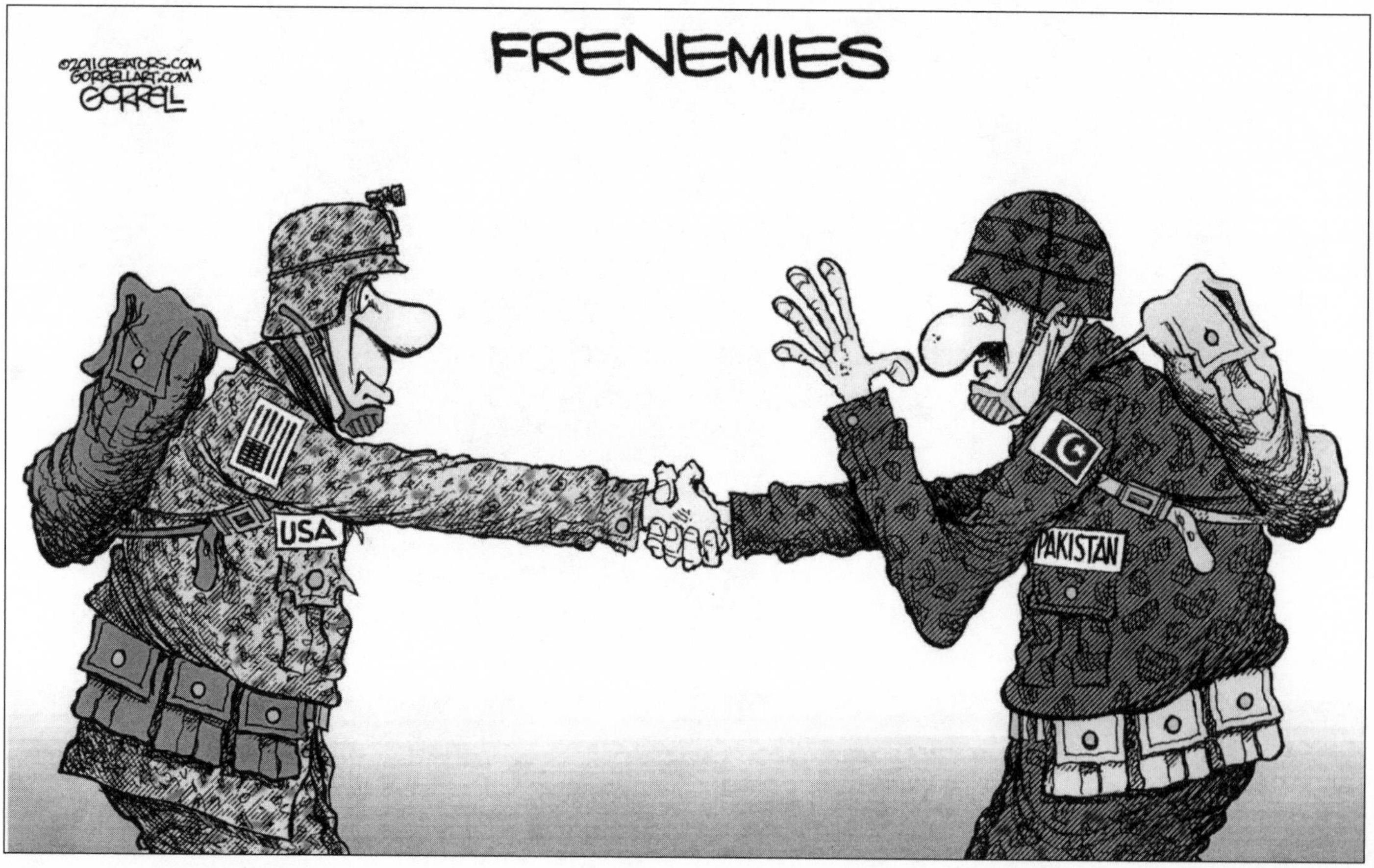
FRENEMIES
©2011 CREATORS.COM
GORRELLART.COM
GORRELL
USA
PAKISTAN

The Class Divide

The Occupy Wall Street movement marked the end of its first year in late 2012. While the motley assortment of protesters did not attract much news coverage at first, they soon became a media favorite and were welcomed by liberals such as former House Speaker Nancy Pelosi. The movement, a loosely organized protest against the capitalist establishment, was called revolutionary and compared to the Arab Spring, uprisings that led to the overthrow of several Middle Eastern and African dictators. It called attention to economic inequality with the chant, "We are the 99 percent."

Protesters first took up lodging in Zuccotti Park in New York, and the movement soon spread to cities worldwide. The bright picture was tarnished, however, by squalid conditions in the Occupy camps, conflicts with the police, and acts of violence within the camps. The movement was without a clear purpose, and those involved made a point of insisting that it had no leader. The ranks of intellectually motivated idealists were soon infiltrated by rootless vagabonds and anarchists. The movement slowly began to disintegrate and devolved into a gathering of homeless individuals.

On the first anniversary of its beginnings, 185 people were arrested when they tried to block access to the New York Stock Exchange. Although greatly diminished in numbers and power, the Occupy Wall Street movement continued to push for economic equity and change in financial institutions.

CLAY BENNETT
Courtesy Chattanooga Times-Free Press

JEFF STAHLER
Courtesy GOCOMICS.COM

MIKE BECKOM
Courtesy beckomtoonz@aol.com

DARYL CAGLE
Courtesy Cagle Cartoons

STEVE GREENBERG
Courtesy Ventura County Reporter (Calif.)

NATE BEELER
Courtesy Washington Examiner

DAVID HORSEY
Courtesy Los Angeles Times

STEVE GREENBERG
Courtesy Ventura County Reporter (Calif.)

MALCOLM MAYES
Courtesy Edmonton Journal (Can.)

NATE BEELER
Courtesy Washington Examiner

CLAY BENNETT
Courtesy Chattanooga Times-Free Press

ROB ROGERS
Courtesy Pittsburgh Post-Gazette

NATE BEELER
Courtesy Washington Examiner

Social Issues

In spite of President Obama's call for moderation in the nation's political discourse, many issues continued to expose deep divides in American society: gay marriage, abortion, gun rights, contraception, drugs, health care, and immigration reform, to name a few.

The head of Chick-fil-A stirred controversy when, in an interview with the *Baptist Press,* he said his company supports "the Biblical definition of the family unit." Liberal activists threatened to boycott the company, and several politicians announced they would try to block expansion of the franchise in their cities. Conservatives organized counter-demonstrations, lining up at Chick-fil-A restaurants across the country to feast on chicken sandwiches.

Florida's Stand Your Ground law came into focus when a Neighborhood Watch volunteer, George Zimmerman, allegedly shot and killed an unarmed black teenager, Trayvon Martin. Zimmerman maintained it was self defense. Missouri Rep. Todd Akin, the GOP candidate for the U.S. Senate in Missouri, embarrassed himself and his party by insisting that a woman's body could block pregnancy after a "legitimate rape." Radio talk show host Rush Limbaugh referred to a birth control activist as a "slut" after she testified before Congress and called for taxpayer funding of contraceptives. An MSNBC commentator also used the "slut" insult against a Fox analyst.

Democrats charged Republicans with waging a "war on women."

DARYL CAGLE
Courtesy Cagle Cartoons

JEN SORENSEN
Courtesy Jen Sorensen

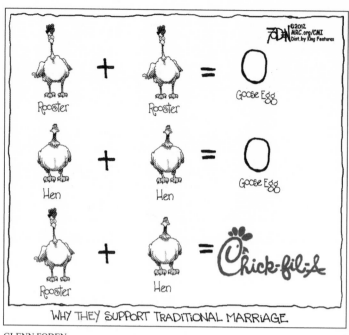

GLENN FODEN
Courtesy King Features

JEFFREY DARCY
Courtesy The Plain Dealer (Oh.)

ROB ROGERS
Courtesy Pittsburgh Post-Gazette

MIKE PETERS
Courtesy Dayton Daily News

JIMMY MARGULIES
Courtesy The Record (N.J.)

JACK OHMAN
Courtesy The Oregonian

STEVE KELLEY
Courtesy The Times-Picayune (La.)

CHAN LOWE
Courtesy South Florida Sun-Sentinel

JOSEPH HOFFECKER
Courtesy American City Business Journals

J.D. CROWE
Courtesy The Press-Register (Ala.)

JOHN COLE
Courtesy The Times-Tribune (Pa.)

CHARLES BEYL
Courtesy The Sunday News (Pa.)

CLAY BENNETT
Courtesy Chattanooga Times-Free Press

ADAM ZYGLIS
Courtesy Buffalo News

GLENN MCCOY
Courtesy BND Uclick

JEFF PARKER
Courtesy Florida Today

JOEL PETT
Courtesy Lexington Herald-Leader

TOM STIGLICH
Courtesy Northeast Times

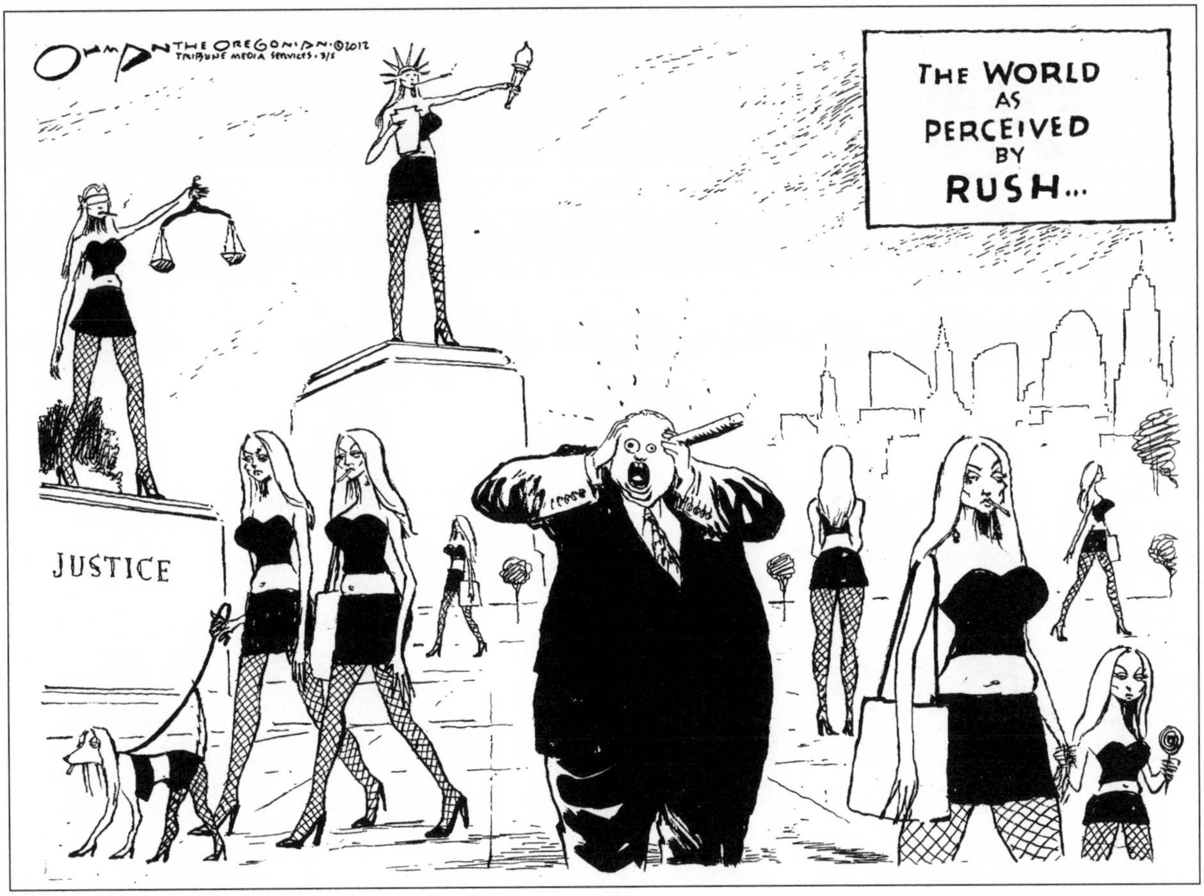
THE WORLD AS PERCEIVED BY RUSH...
JUSTICE

JACK OHMAN
Courtesy The Oregonian

JOE HELLER
Courtesy Green Bay Press-Gazette

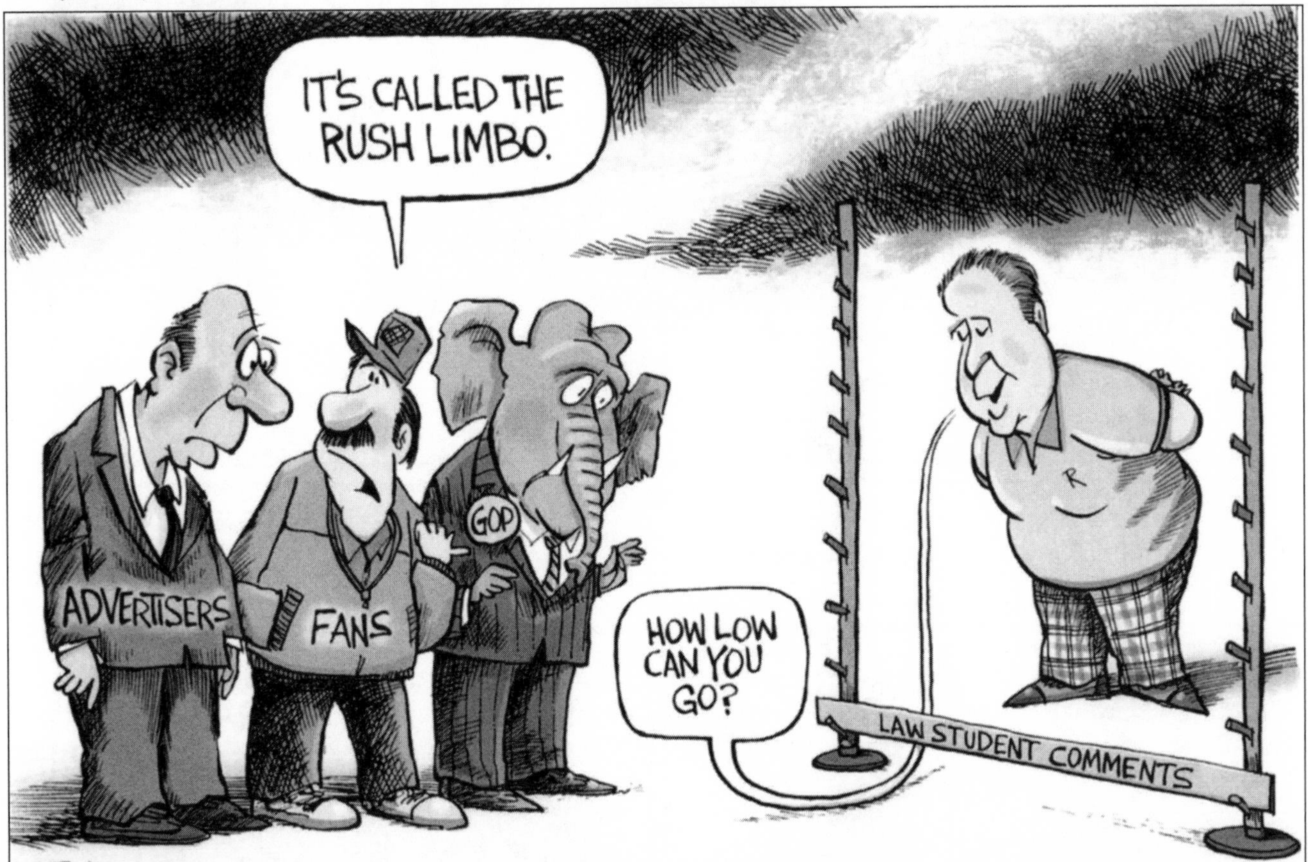
IT'S CALLED THE RUSH LIMBO.
ADVERTISERS
FANS
GOP
HOW LOW CAN YOU GO?
LAW STUDENT COMMENTS

ED HALL
Courtesy Artizans Syndicate

MATT WUERKER
Courtesy Politico

GARY VARVEL
Courtesy Indianapolis Star

MIKE PETERS
Courtesy Dayton Daily News

ROB ROGERS
Courtesy Pittsburgh Post-Gazette

NICK ANDERSON
Courtesy Houston Chronicle

JACK OHMAN
Courtesy The Oregonian

KEVIN SIERS
Courtesy Charlotte Observer

MIKE PETERS
Courtesy Dayton Daily News

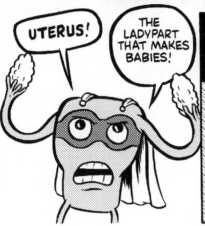

MATT BORS
Courtesy Universal Uclick

JIMMY MARGULIES
Courtesy The Record (N.J.)

143

caglecartoons.com

TAYLOR JONES
Courtesy Cagle Cartoons

RICK MCKEE
Courtesy Augusta Chronicle

MIKE PETERS
Courtesy Dayton Daily News

NICK ANDERSON
Courtesy Houston Chronicle

ROB ROGERS
Courtesy Pittsburgh Post-Gazette

CLAY BENNETT
Courtesy Chattanooga Times-Free Press

146

The Environment

The debate over global warming continues, although polls show most Americans now believe the problem is real. Another poll, however, shows that air and water pollution are a bigger concern.

With gas prices continuing to surge, most voters believe the nation should invest in renewable energy sources such as wind and solar energy, rather than fossil fuels. The government has invested heavily in the Chevy Volt hybrid car, but it showed an unfortunate tendency to catch fire itself, rather than with the public. In crash tests, the battery was found to be the source of fires. The $40,000 price tag may be part of the reason for slow sales. General Motors has offered to either replace the Volt with another GM car or buy the Volt back from skittish owners.

Most Americans feel plans for the Keystone pipeline project should go forward, despite strong opposition from environmentalists, who warn it could pollute air and water supplies and harm wildlife. The pipeline would deliver oil from Canadian oil sands to terminals in the U.S.

Another energy controversy involves fracking, a method of introducing pressurized liquids into rock formations to facilitate production of fossil fuels, primarily natural gas. The increased production has caused natural gas prices to drop precipitously, offering hope for an alternative to dirtier fossil fuels such as coal and oil.

MIKE LUCKOVICH
Courtesy Atlanta Journal-Constitution

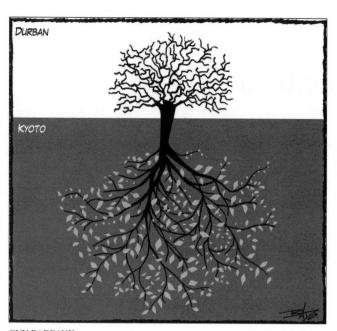

GUY BADEAUX
Courtesy LeDroit (Ottawa)

DAVID FITZSIMMONS
Courtesy Arizona Daily Star

STEVEN G. ARTLEY
Courtesy artleytoons.com

STEPHANIE MCMILLAN
Courtesy Code Green

MICHAEL RAMIREZ
Investor's Business Daily

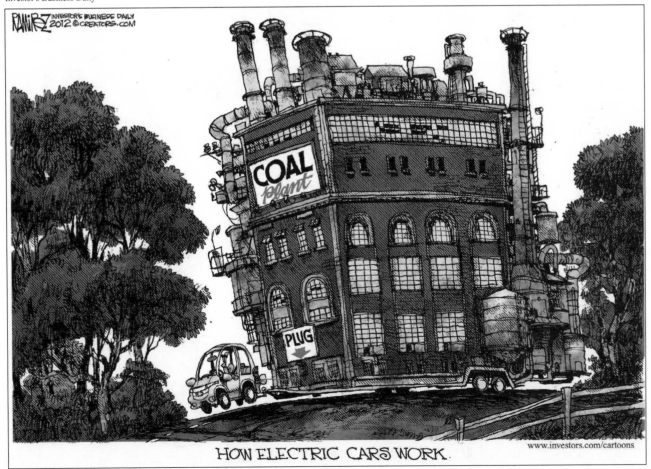

149

GLENN FODEN
Courtesy King Features

CHIP BOK
Courtesy Creators Syndicate

STEPHANIE MCMILLAN
Courtesy Code Green

MICHAEL RAMIREZ
Investor's Business Daily

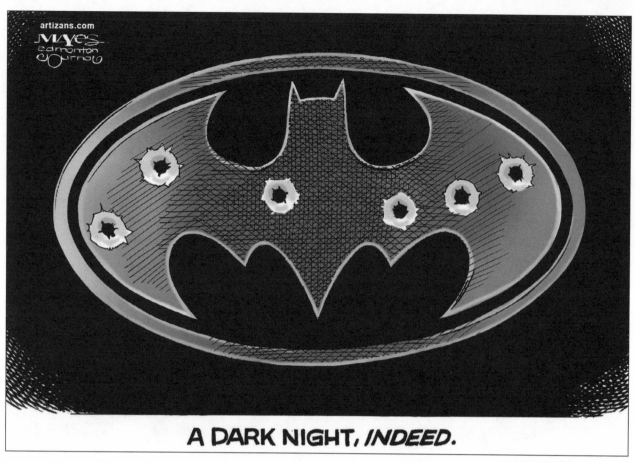

A DARK NIGHT, *INDEED.*

MALCOLM MAYES
Courtesy Edmonton Journal (Can.)

ROBERT ENGLEHART
Courtesy Hartford Courant

Gun Violence

The largest mass shooting in U.S. history occurred in Aurora, Colorado, during a sold-out premiere of the new Batman movie, "The Dark Knight Rises." A twenty-four-year-old honors student and Ph.D. candidate allegedly emptied four weapons into the movie crowd, killing twelve and wounding dozens. Victims and their families will receive about $175,000 each from $5 million in donations.

The horrific incident predictably renewed calls for stricter gun control laws and, just as predictably, pushback from gun owners and the National Rifle Association, a lobbying powerhouse.

Neighborhood Watch volunteer George Zimmerman allegedly shot and killed an unarmed black teenager in Sanford, Florida. Zimmerman claimed he acted in self-defense, after the youth attacked him. Zimmerman was not immediately arrested, sparking protests. A special prosecutor charged Zimmerman with second-degree murder. Fox News analyst Geraldo Rivera suggested that a contributing factor in the teen's death might have been the hoodie he was wearing. Hoodies presumably are popular garments among some gangsters.

TOM STIGLICH
Courtesy Northeast Times

A DARK NIGHT

MEANINGFUL GUN REFORM LEGISLATION

NRA

SILENCER...

ADAM ZYGLIS
Courtesy Buffalo News

DAVID DONAR
Courtesy David Donar

JEFF STAHLER
Courtesy GOCOMICS.COM

BETTER GUN CONTROL

CONGRESS

VOTE ME

STAHLER.
GOCOMICS.COM 2012

JOEL PETT
Courtesy Lexington Herald-Leader

RANDY BISH
Courtesy Pittsburgh Tribune-Review

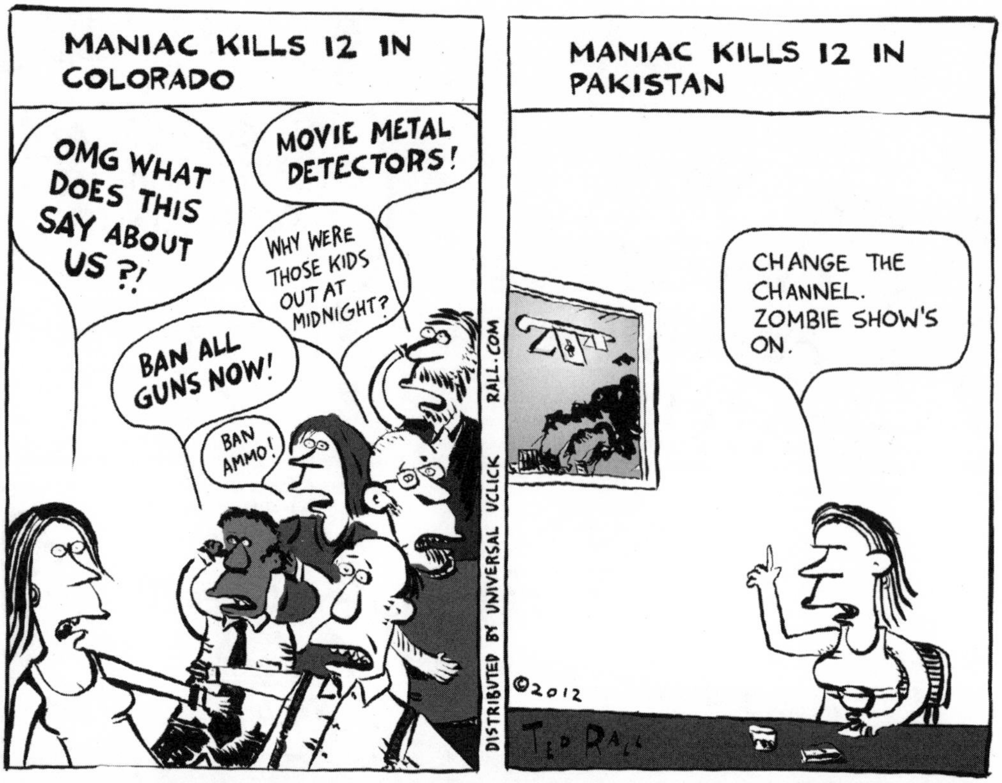
MANIAC KILLS 12 IN COLORADO
OMG WHAT DOES THIS SAY ABOUT US ?!
MOVIE METAL DETECTORS!
WHY WERE THOSE KIDS OUT AT MIDNIGHT?
BAN ALL GUNS NOW!
BAN AMMO!
DISTRIBUTED BY UNIVERSAL UCLICK RALL.COM
MANIAC KILLS 12 IN PAKISTAN
CHANGE THE CHANNEL. ZOMBIE SHOW'S ON.
©2012
TED RALL

TED RALL
Courtesy Universal Uclick

DARYL CAGLE
Courtesy Cagle Cartoons

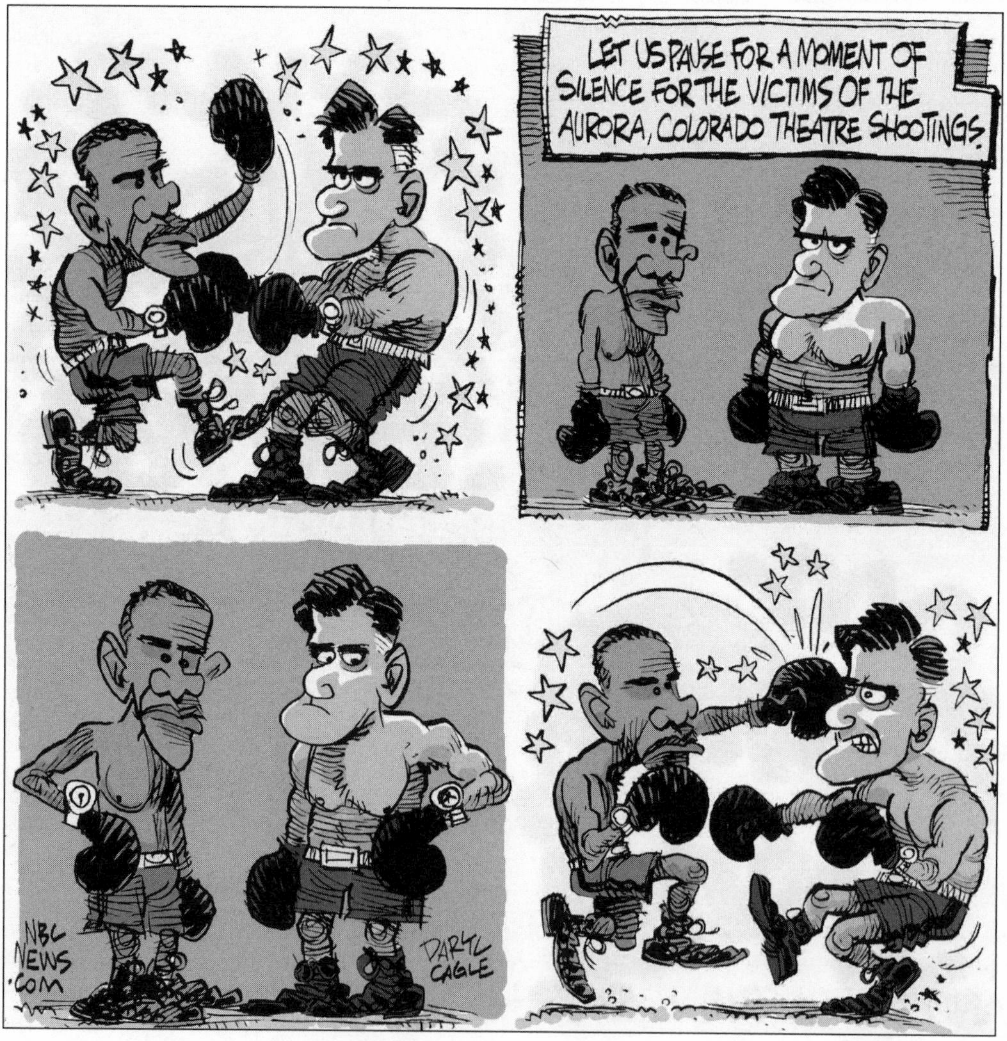
LET US PAUSE FOR A MOMENT OF SILENCE FOR THE VICTIMS OF THE AURORA, COLORADO THEATRE SHOOTINGS.
NBC NEWS .COM
DARYL CAGLE

MIKE PETERS
Courtesy Dayton Daily News

NICK ANDERSON
Courtesy Houston Chronicle

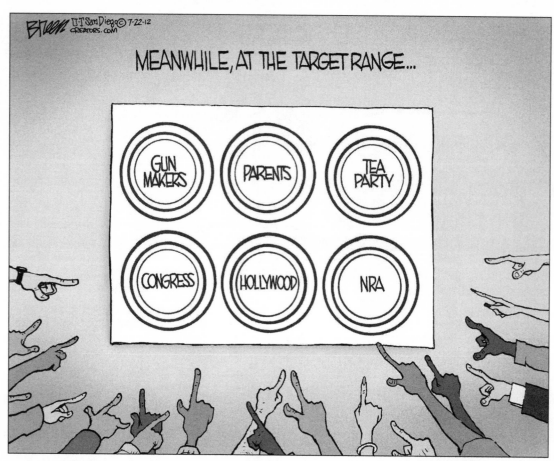

STEVE BREEN
Courtesy San Diego Union-Tribune

CHIP BOK
Courtesy Creators Syndicate

JESSE SPRINGER
Courtesy Springer Creative

TOM STIGLICH
Courtesy Northeast Times

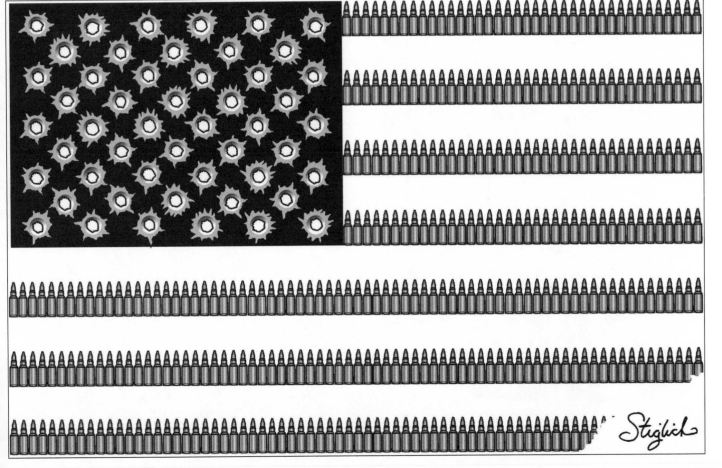

STEVE KELLEY
Courtesy The Times-Picayune (La.)

STEVE LINDSTROM
Courtesy Duluth News-Tribune

STEVE BREEN
Courtesy San Diego Union-Tribune

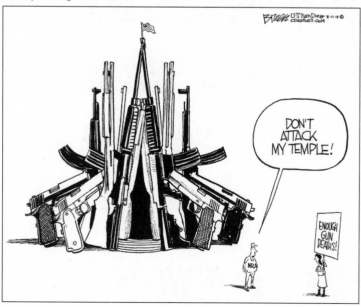

MIKE LUCKOVICH
Courtesy Atlanta Journal-Constitution

DAVID FITZSIMMONS
Courtesy Arizona Daily Star

MIKE LESTER
Courtesy Washington Post Writers Group

MIKE KEEFE
Courtesy Denver Post

MIKE LUCKOVICH
Courtesy Atlanta Journal-Constitution

ROB ROGERS
Courtesy Pittsburgh Post-Gazette

JEN SORENSEN
Courtesy Jen Sorensen

CHARLES BEYL
Courtesy The Sunday News (Pa.

JIM MORIN
Courtesy Miami Herald

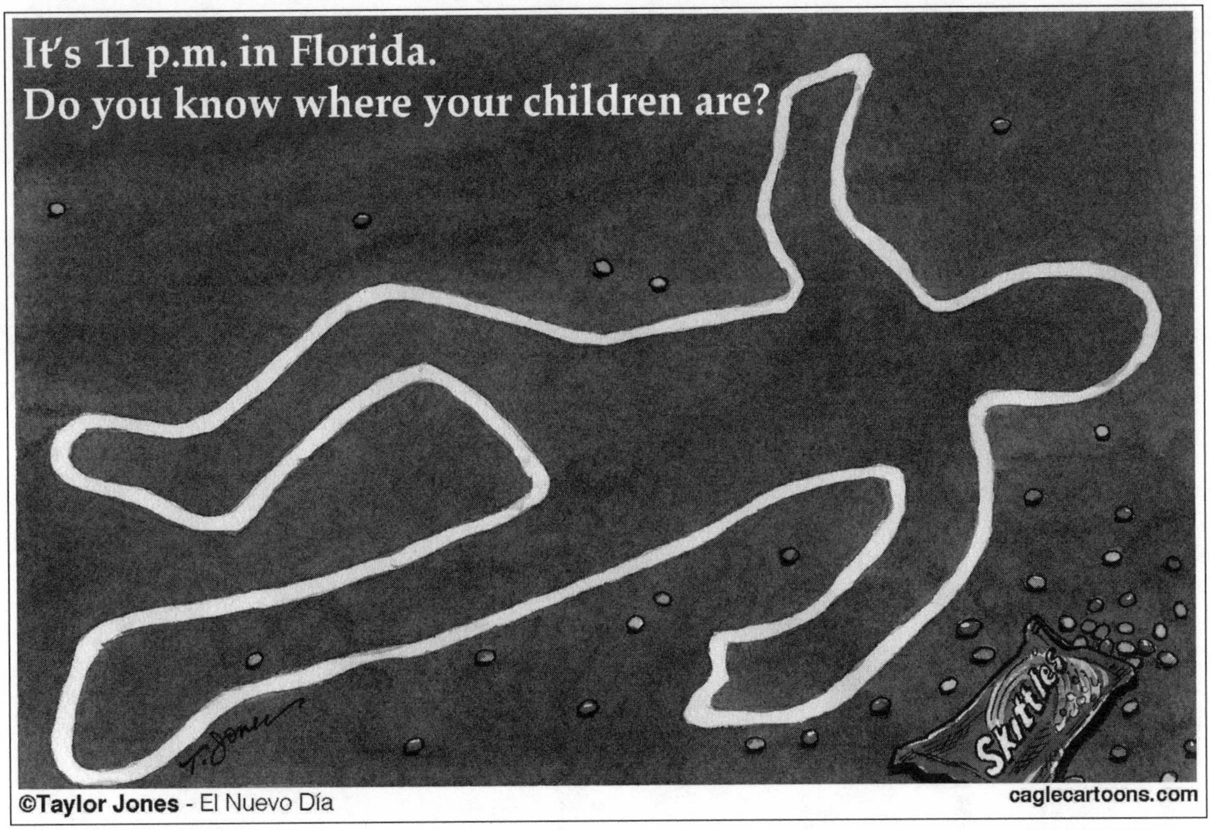
It's 11 p.m. in Florida.
Do you know where your children are?
Skittles
©Taylor Jones - El Nuevo Día
caglecartoons.com

TAYLOR JONES
Courtesy Cagle Cartoons

CHRIS BRITT
Courtesy State Journal-Register (Ill.)

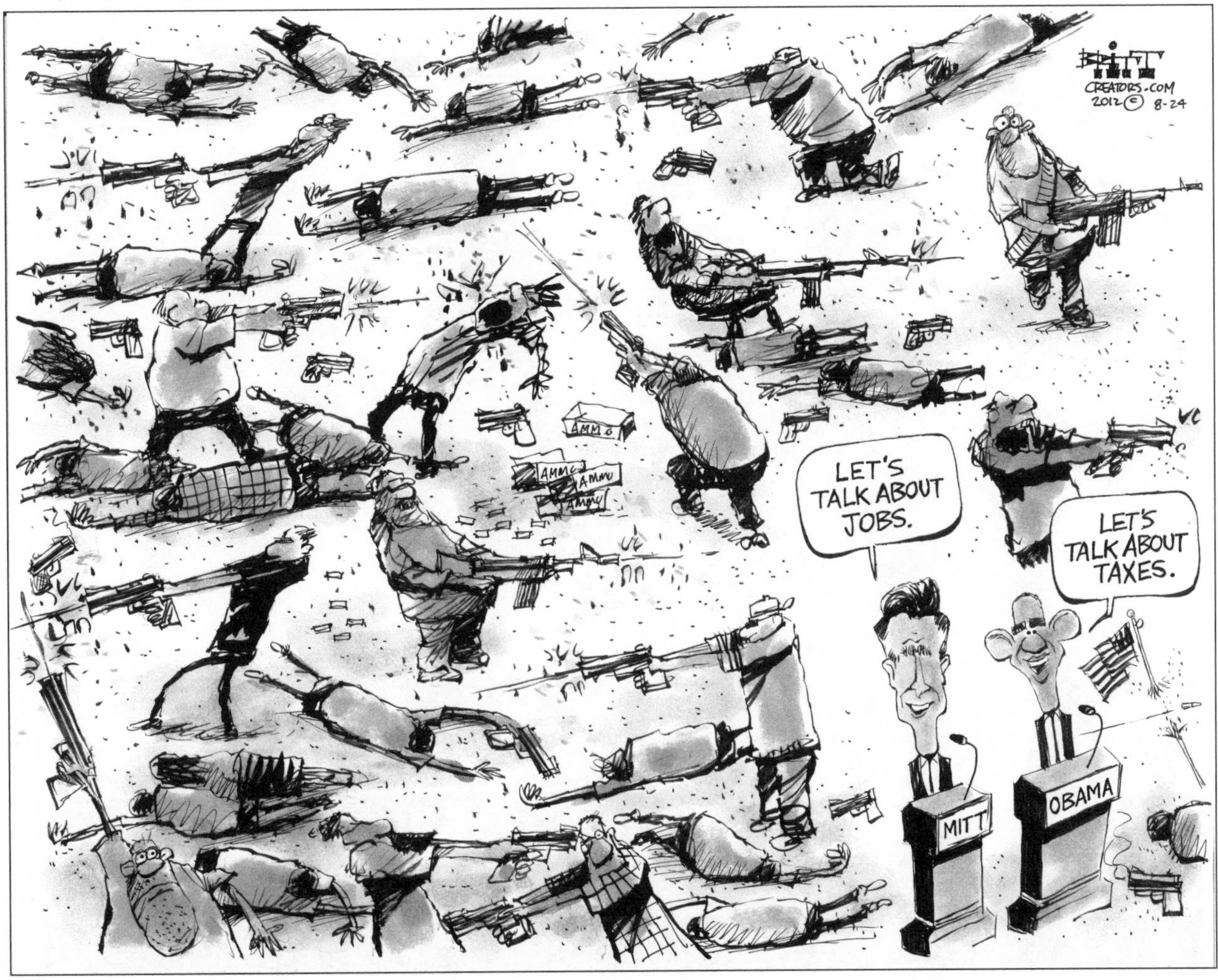
CREATORS.COM
2012 © 8-24
AMMO
LET'S TALK ABOUT JOBS.
LET'S TALK ABOUT TAXES.
MITT
OBAMA

MIKE LUCKOVICH
Courtesy Atlanta Journal-Constitution

Penn State

The biggest scandal in the history of Penn State University resulted in the conviction of former assistant football coach Jerry Sandusky on forty-five counts of molesting ten young boys over a period of fifteen years. He was sentenced to 30-60 years in prison. Sandusky met the boys through a foundation he created for underprivileged children. School President Graham Spanier was forced to resign.

The scandal also touched legendary football coach Joe Paterno, who was accused of knowing about the abuse and doing little to stop it. An assistant coach who saw Sandusky in the shower with a boy reported it to Paterno, and Paterno reported it to his superior and campus police, fulfilling the letter of the law. But general public sentiment held that both of them should have done more when it became clear that university officials were not going to act.

Paterno was disgraced and fired, and a statue of him on campus was taken down. Nevertheless, some 4,000 rallied in his support. He died of lung cancer two months later.

The scandal has had far-reaching consequences for the institution. The NCAA imposed sweeping penalties on the university, including a fine of $60 million and a four-year postseason ban. In addition, all victories from 1998 through 2011 were vacated. The Big Ten Conference subsequently punished the university with an additional $13 million fine.

MARC MURPHY
Courtesy Louisville Courier-Journal

RANDY BISH
Courtesy Pittsburgh Tribune-Review

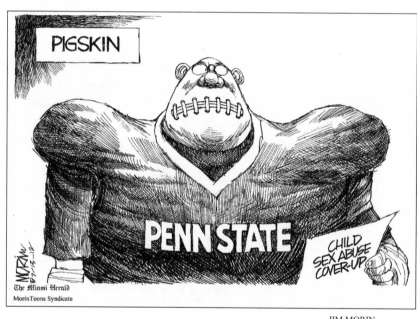

JIM MORIN
Courtesy Miami Herald

JEFFREY DARCY
Courtesy The Plain Dealer (Oh.)

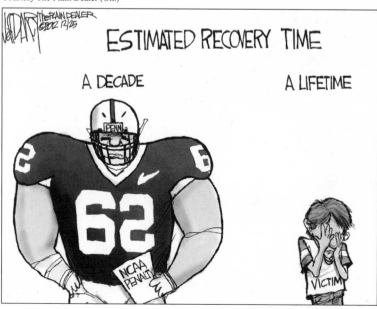

BRUCE PLANTE
Courtesy Tulsa World

NICK ANDERSON
Courtesy Houston Chronicle

JAKE FULLER
Courtesy Artizans Syndicate

JOHN COLE
Courtesy The Times-Tribune (Pa.)

DAVID FITZSIMMONS
Courtesy Arizona Daily Star

J.D. CROWE
Courtesy The Press-Register (Ala.)

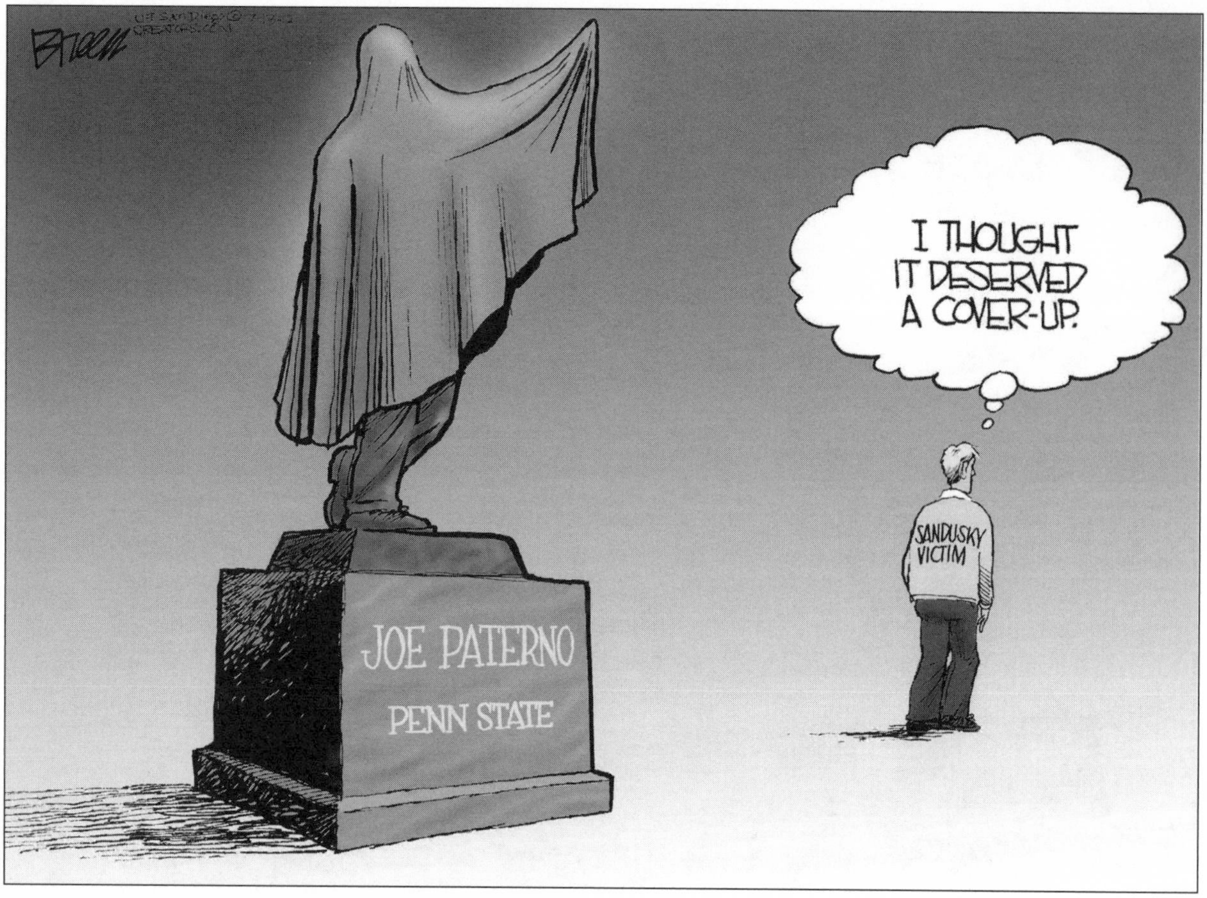
BREEN
I THOUGHT IT DESERVED A COVER-UP.
SANDUSKY VICTIM
JOE PATERNO
PENN STATE

STEVE BREEN
Courtesy San Diego Union-Tribune

NATE BEELER
Courtesy Columbus Dispatch

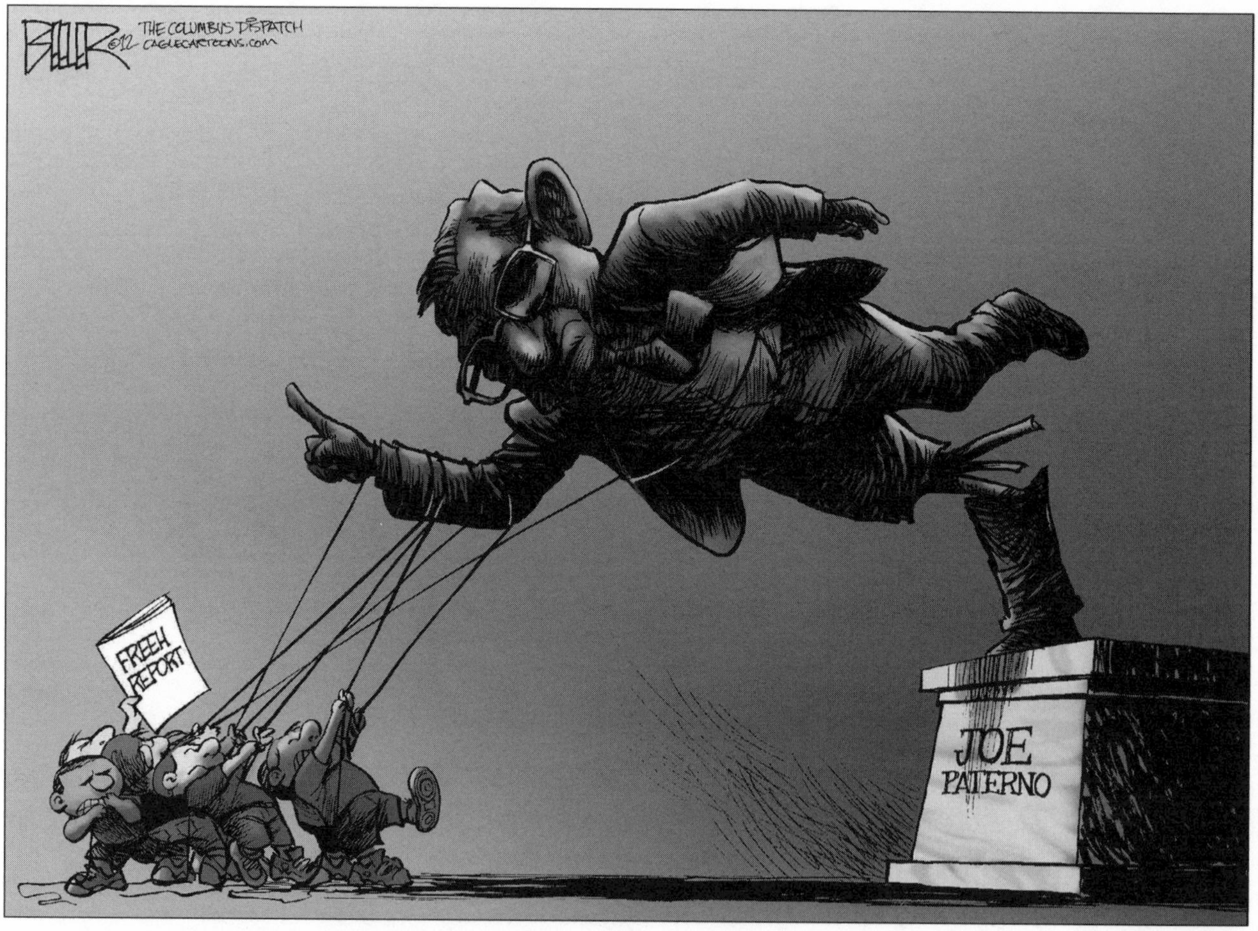
BEELER
THE COLUMBUS DISPATCH
FREEH REPORT
JOE PATERNO

Social Media

American society is becoming highly digitized. Computers and smart phones have invaded virtually every aspect of modern life. More and more people, especially the younger generation, are turning from print newspapers, landline telephones, and television, preferring online services such as Twitter, Facebook, and LinkedIn. Newspapers are publishing online, cutting back on delivering print. After 79 years of publishing, *Newsweek* announced it was ending its print operation in favor of digital. Many computer functions and services are now conducted on the internet (cloud computing).

Facebook, the most popular social medium, went public in May and sold more than 421 million shares, raising $16 billion. By August, however, the stock had lost half of its opening market value.

Computers such as iPads and other tablets are getting smaller and handier, and run applications to deal with almost every imaginable daily need. Cars now come fitted with GPS, satellite radio, rear-view cameras, and automatic parking. Three states, Nevada, Florida, and California, have approved the operation of driverless cars that navigate by computer.

The digital revolution is not without a downside. Texting while driving has become as dangerous as driving while intoxicated.

J.D. CROWE
Courtesy The Press-Register (Ala.)

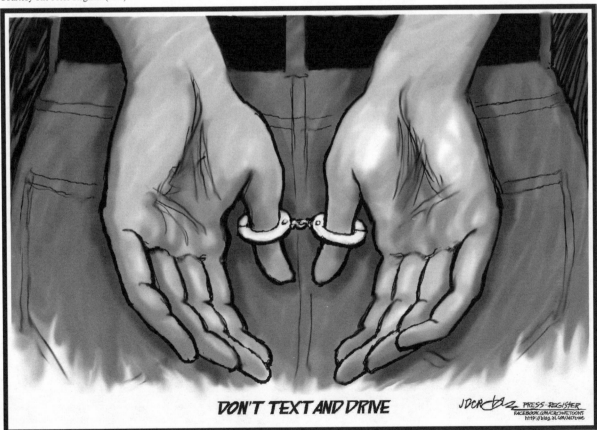

DON'T TEXT AND DRIVE

JIM MORIN
Courtesy Miami Herald

DEB MILBRATH
Courtesy Deb Milbrath

JOSEPH HOFFECKER
Courtesy American City Business Journals

DAVID HORSEY
Courtesy Los Angeles Times

GEORGE DANBY
Courtesy Bangor Daily News

GUY BADEAUX
Courtesy LeDroit (Ottawa)

BOB GORRELL
Courtesy Gorrell Creative

JEFF STAHLER
Courtesy Universal Uclick

JOEL PETT
Courtesy Lexington Herald-Leader

177

KARL WIMER
Courtesy Denver Business Journal

JEN SORENSEN
Courtesy Jen Sorensen

DANIEL FENECH
Courtesy Heritage Newspapers / Journal Register Co.

WALT HANDELSMAN
Courtesy Newsday

MIKE KEEFE
Courtesy Denver Post

STEVE NEASE
Courtesy Nease Cartoons

JOSEPH HOFFECKER
Courtesy American City Business Journals

ANN CLEAVES
Courtesy Ann Cleaves

ROGER SCHILLERSTROM
Courtesy Crain Communications

JIMMY MARGULIES
Courtesy The Record (N.J.)

"I WAS DISTRACTED BY A PHONE APP THAT LETS ME KNOW WHERE THE SPEED TRAPS ARE..."

DANIEL FENECH
Courtesy Heritage Newspapers / Journal Register Co.

JIM SIERGEY
Courtesy jimsiergey.com

In Memoriam

A number of notables died during the past year, including:

—Steve Jobs, founder of Apple. The charismatic entrepreneur gave the world the iMac, iTunes, iPod, iPhone, and iPad.

—Andy Griffith, actor, producer, gospel singer, and writer. He is best known for his television role as the sheriff of Mayberry in "The Andy Griffith Show."

—Dick Clark, host of America's longest-running variety program, "American Bandstand."

—Mike Wallace, a journalist. He was one of the original correspondents for CBS' "60 Minutes," which began in 1968.

—Neil Armstrong, astronaut, the first person to walk on the moon.

—Maurice Sendak, a writer and illustrator of children's literature. He is best known for his book *Where the Wild Things Are.*

—Sally Ride, astronaut, the first American woman in space.

STEVEN PARRA
Courtesy Fresno Bee

BOB KRIEGER
Courtesy The Province (Can.)

JEFFREY DARCY
Courtesy The Plain Dealer (Oh.)

JEFFREY DARCY
Courtesy The Plain Dealer (Oh.)

JIMMY MARGULIES
Courtesy The Record (N.J.)

STEVEN PARRA
Courtesy Fresno Bee

TOM STIGLICH
Courtesy Northeast Times

Sally Ride
1951-2012

... and Other Issues

The news that Secret Service agents drank heavily and brought prostitutes to their rooms on a foreign trip tarnished the image of the corps responsible for protecting the U.S. president. The agents were in Colombia in advance of a visit by President Obama.

Profligate spending by the General Services Administration led to a congressional investigation of more than 77 conferences and award ceremonies. The GSA spent more than $800,000 for a convention in Las Vegas, and treated 120 interns to a five-day conference in Palm Springs, Calif.

Some Boy Scouts and their leaders began speaking out against the organization's ban on members who are openly gay. President Obama and Mitt Romney both oppose the ban. The Augusta National Golf Club admitted its first two female members, Condoleezza Rice and Darla Moore. Michael Phelps became the most decorated Olympic athlete of all time, winning his 22nd medal at the 2012 Games in London.

The U.S. Federal Aviation Administration expects 30,000 commercial and government drones to be flying over U.S. airspace within twenty years, raising concerns about privacy. The drones are cheap, can be as small as an insect, and are able to stay aloft indefinitely.

Vladimir Putin was reelected to a third term as president of Russia with a reported 64 percent of the vote. Thousands protested in Moscow, alleging election fraud.

TIM CAMPBELL
Courtesy Current Publishing

GRAEME MACKAY
Courtesy Hamilton Spectator (Can.)

JEFF PARKER
Courtesy Florida Today

MATT BORS
Courtesy Universal Uclick

ROBERT ENGLEHART
Courtesy Hartford Courant

MALCOLM MAYES
Courtesy Edmonton Journal (Can.)

BRUCE MACKINNON
Courtesy Halifax Chronicle-Herald (N.S.)

MATT BORS
Courtesy Universal Uclick

CHIP BOK
Courtesy Creators Syndicate

MIKE KEEFE
Courtesy Denver Post

JEFF PARKER
Courtesy Florida Today

DAVID BROWN
Courtesy David Brown Studios

ROBERT ENGLEHART
Courtesy Hartford Courant

192

JOEL PETT
Courtesy Lexington Herald-Leader

STEVEN G. ARTLEY
Courtesy artleytoons.com

CHAN LOWE
Courtesy South Florida Sun-Sentinel

CHRIS BRITT
Courtesy State Journal-Register (Ill.)

ROBERT ARIAIL
Courtesy Spartanburg Herald-Journal

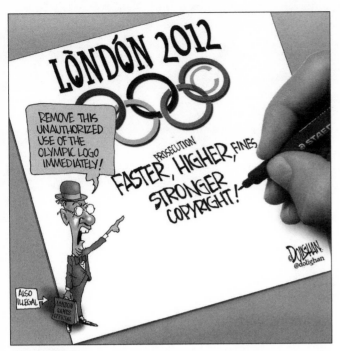

TIM DOLIGHAN
Courtesy Dolighan Cartoons

BOB KRIEGER
Courtesy The Province (Can.)

JIMMY MARGULIES
Courtesy The Record (N.J.)

RANDY BISH
Courtesy Pittsburgh Tribune-Review

DAVID HORSEY
Courtesy Los Angeles Times

THEO MOUDAKIS
Courtesy Toronto Star (Can.)

TIM DOLIGHAN
Courtesy Dolighan Cartoons

MIKE LESTER
Courtesy Washington Post Writers Group

MILT PRIGGEE
Courtesy Puget Sound Business Journal

DAVID HORSEY
Courtesy Los Angeles Times

JOHN BRANCH
Courtesy BranchToon.com

JOEL PETT
Courtesy Lexington Herald-Leader

LISA BENSON
Courtesy Washington Post Writers Group

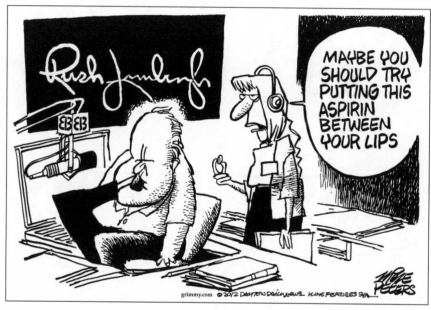

MIKE LESTER
Courtesy Washington Post Writers Group

MIKE PETERS
Courtesy Dayton Daily News

JOHN COLE
Courtesy The Times-Tribune (Pa.)

MIKE GEMPELER
Courtesy Lee's Summit Journal

GARY MARKSTEIN
Courtesy Creators Syndicate

NATE BEELER
Courtesy Columbus Dispatch

NEWS ITEM: LONDON to PUT MISSILES on ROOFTOPS for OLYMPICS SECURITY...

Past Award Winners

PULITZER PRIZE

1922—Rollin Kirby, New York World
1923—No award given
1924—J.N. Darling, New York Herald-Tribune
1925—Rollin Kirby, New York World
1926—D.R. Fitzpatrick, St. Louis Post-Dispatch
1927—Nelson Harding, Brooklyn Eagle
1928—Nelson Harding, Brooklyn Eagle
1929—Rollin Kirby, New York World
1930—Charles Macauley, Brooklyn Eagle
1931—Edmund Duffy, Baltimore Sun
1932—John T. McCutcheon, Chicago Tribune
1933—H.M. Talburt, Washington Daily News
1934—Edmund Duffy, Baltimore Sun
1935—Ross A. Lewis, Milwaukee Journal
1936—No award given
1937—C.D. Batchelor, New York Daily News
1938—Vaughn Shoemaker, Chicago Daily News
1939—Charles G. Werner, Daily Oklahoman
1940—Edmund Duffy, Baltimore Sun
1941—Jacob Burck, Chicago Times
1942—Herbert L. Block, NEA
1943—Jay N. Darling, New York Herald-Tribune
1944—Clifford K. Berryman, Washington Star
1945—Bill Mauldin, United Features Syndicate
1946—Bruce Russell, Los Angeles Times
1947—Vaughn Shoemaker, Chicago Daily News
1948—Reuben L. ("Rube") Goldberg, New York Sun
1949—Lute Pease, Newark Evening News
1950—James T. Berryman, Washington Star
1951—Reginald W. Manning, Arizona Republic
1952—Fred L. Packer, New York Mirror
1953—Edward D. Kuekes, Cleveland Plain Dealer
1954—Herbert L. Block, Washington Post
1955—Daniel R. Fitzpatrick, St. Louis Post-Dispatch
1956—Robert York, Louisville Times
1957—Tom Little, Nashville Tennessean
1958—Bruce M. Shanks, Buffalo Evening News
1959—Bill Mauldin, St. Louis Post-Dispatch
1960—No award given
1961—Carey Orr, Chicago Tribune
1962—Edmund S. Valtman, Hartford Times
1963—Frank Miller, Des Moines Register
1964—Paul Conrad, Denver Post
1965—No award given
1966—Don Wright, Miami News
1967—Patrick B. Oliphant, Denver Post
1968—Eugene Gray Payne, Charlotte Observer

1969—John Fischetti, Chicago Daily News
1970—Thomas F. Darcy, Newsday
1971—Paul Conrad, Los Angeles Times
1972—Jeffrey K. MacNelly, Richmond News Leader
1973—No award given
1974—Paul Szep, Boston Globe
1975—Garry Trudeau, Universal Press Syndicate
1976—Tony Auth, Philadelphia Enquirer
1977—Paul Szep, Boston Globe
1978—Jeff MacNelly, Richmond News Leader
1979—Herbert Block, Washington Post
1980—Don Wright, Miami News
1981—Mike Peters, Dayton Daily News
1982—Ben Sargent, Austin American-Statesman
1983—Dick Locher, Chicago Tribune
1984—Paul Conrad, Los Angeles Times
1985—Jeff MacNelly, Chicago Tribune
1986—Jules Feiffer, Universal Press Syndicate
1987—Berke Breathed, Washington Post Writers Group
1988—Doug Marlette, Atlanta Constitution
1989—Jack Higgins, Chicago Sun-Times
1990—Tom Toles, Buffalo News
1991—Jim Borgman, Cincinnati Enquirer
1992—Signe Wilkinson, Philadelphia Daily News
1993—Steve Benson, Arizona Republic
1994—Michael Ramirez, Memphis Commercial Appeal
1995—Mike Luckovich, Atlanta Constitution
1996—Jim Morin, Miami Herald
1997—Walt Handelsman, New Orleans Times-Picayune
1998—Steve Breen, Asbury Park Press
1999—David Horsey, Seattle Post-Intelligencer
2000—Joel Pett, Lexington Herald-Leader
2001—Ann Telnaes, Tribune Media Services
2002—Clay Bennett, Christian Science Monitor
2003—David Horsey, Seattle Post-Intelligencer
2004—Matt Davies, The Journal News
2005—Nick Anderson, Louisville Courier-Journal
2006—Mike Luckovich, Atlanta Journal-Constitution
2007—Walt Handelsman, Newsday
2008—Michael Ramirez, Investors Business Daily
2009—Steve Breen, San Diego Tribune
2010—Mark Fiore, SFGate.com
2011—Mike Keefe, Denver Post
2012—Matt Wuerker, Politico

SIGMA DELTA CHI AWARD

1942—Jacob Burck, Chicago Times
1943—Charles Werner, Chicago Sun
1944—Henry Barrow, Associated Press
1945—Reuben L. Goldberg, New York Sun
1946—Dorman H. Smith, NEA
1947—Bruce Russell, Los Angeles Times
1948—Herbert Block, Washington Post
1949—Herbert Block, Washington Post
1950—Bruce Russell, Los Angeles Times
1951—Herbert Block, Washington Post and
        Bruce Russell, Los Angeles Times
1952—Cecil Jensen, Chicago Daily News
1953—John Fischetti, NEA
1954—Calvin Alley, Memphis Commercial Appeal
1955—John Fischetti, NEA
1956—Herbert Block, Washington Post
1957—Scott Long, Minneapolis Tribune
1958—Clifford H. Baldowski, Atlanta Constitution
1959—Charles G. Brooks, Birmingham News
1960—Dan Dowling, New York Herald-Tribune
1961—Frank Interlandi, Des Moines Register
1962—Paul Conrad, Denver Post
1963—William Mauldin, Chicago Sun-Times
1964—Charles Bissell, Nashville Tennessean
1965—Roy Justus, Minneapolis Star
1966—Patrick Oliphant, Denver Post
1967—Eugene Payne, Charlotte Observer
1968—Paul Conrad, Los Angeles Times
1969—William Mauldin, Chicago Sun-Times
1970—Paul Conrad, Los Angeles Times
1971—Hugh Haynie, Louisville Courier-Journal
1972—William Mauldin, Chicago Sun-Times
1973—Paul Szep, Boston Globe
1974—Mike Peters, Dayton Daily News
1975—Tony Auth, Philadelphia Enquirer
1976—Paul Szep, Boston Globe

1977—Don Wright, Miami News
1978—Jim Borgman, Cincinnati Enquirer
1979—John P. Trever, Albuquerque Journal
1980—Paul Conrad, Los Angeles Times
1981—Paul Conrad, Los Angeles Times
1982—Dick Locher, Chicago Tribune
1983—Rob Lawlor, Philadelphia Daily News
1984—Mike Lane, Baltimore Evening Sun
1985—Doug Marlette, Charlotte Observer
1986—Mike Keefe, Denver Post
1987—Paul Conrad, Los Angeles Times
1988—Jack Higgins, Chicago Sun-Times
1989—Don Wright, Palm Beach Post
1990—Jeff MacNelly, Chicago Tribune
1991—Walt Handelsman, New Orleans Times-
        Picayune
1992—Robert Ariail, Columbia State
1993—Herbert Block, Washington Post
1994—Jim Borgman, Cincinnati Enquirer
1995—Michael Ramirez, Memphis Commercial
        Appeal
1996—Paul Conrad, Los Angeles Times
1997—Michael Ramirez, Los Angeles Times
1998—Jack Higgins, Chicago Sun-Times
1999—Mike Thompson, Detroit Free Press
2000—Nick Anderson, Louisville Courier-Journal
2001—Clay Bennett, Christian Science Monitor
2002—Mike Thompson, Detroit Free Press
2003—Steve Sack, Minneapolis Star-Tribune
2004—John Sherffius, jsherffius@aol.com
2005—Mike Luckovich, Atlanta Journal-Constitution
2006—Mike Lester, Rome News-Tribune
2007—Michael Ramirez, Investors Business Daily
2008—Chris Britt, State Journal-Register
2009—Jack Ohman, The Oregonian
2010—Stephanie McMillan, Code Green
2011—Matt Bors, Universal Uclick

Index of Cartoonists

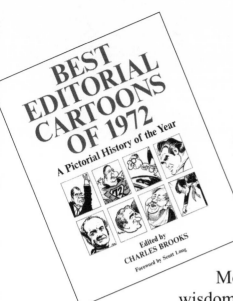

Complete Your
CARTOON
COLLECTION

Previous editions of this timeless
classic are available for those
wishing to update their
collection of the most
provocative moments
of the past four decades.
Most important, in the end, the wit and
wisdom of the editorial cartoonists prevail on the
pages of these opinion editorials, where one can find memories
and much, much more in the work of the nation's finest cartoonists.

Select from the following supply of past editions

_____1972 Edition	$20.00 pb (F)	_____1987 Edition	$20.00 pb	_____2001 Edition	$20.00 pb
_____1974 Edition	$20.00 pb (F)	_____1988 Edition	$20.00 pb	_____2002 Edition	$14.95 pb
_____1975 Edition	$20.00 pb (F)	_____1989 Edition	$20.00 pb (F)	_____2003 Edition	$14.95 pb
_____1976 Edition	$20.00 pb (F)	_____1990 Edition	$20.00 pb	_____2004 Edition	$14.95 pb
_____1977 Edition	$20.00 pb (F)	_____1991 Edition	$20.00 pb	_____2005 Edition	$14.95 pb
_____1978 Edition	$20.00 pb (F)	_____1992 Edition	$20.00 pb	_____2006 Edition	$14.95 pb
_____1979 Edition	$20.00 pb (F)	_____1993 Edition	$20.00 pb	_____2007 Edition	$14.95 pb
_____1980 Edition	$20.00 pb (F)	_____1994 Edition	$20.00 pb	_____2008 Edition	$14.95 pb
_____1981 Edition	$20.00 pb (F)	_____1995 Edition	$20.00 pb	_____2009 Edition	$14.95 pb
_____1982 Edition	$20.00 pb (F)	_____1996 Edition	$20.00 pb	_____2010 Edition	$14.95 pb
_____1983 Edition	$20.00 pb (F)	_____1997 Edition	$20.00 pb	_____2011 Edition	$14.95 pb
_____1984 Edition	$20.00 pb (F)	_____1998 Edition	$20.00 pb	_____2012 Edition	$14.95 pb
_____1985 Edition	$20.00 pb (F)	_____1999 Edition	$20.00 pb	_____Add me to the list of standing	
_____1986 Edition	$20.00 pb (F)	_____2000 Edition	$20.00 pb	orders	

TO PLACE AN ORDER
CALL 1-800-843-1724,
visit our Web site at www.pelicanpub.com, or
e-mail us at sales@pelicanpub.com